Are World Population Trends A Problem?

Edited, with an Introduction, by
Ben Wattenberg
and Karl Zinsmeister

American Enterprise Institute for Public Policy Research
Washington, D.C.

Papers and comments by conference participants have been edited.
The American Enterprise Institute for Public Policy Research, established in 1943, is a nonpartisan research and educational organization supported by foundations, corporations, and the public at large. Its purpose is to assist policy makers, scholars, businessmen, the press, and the public by providing objective analysis of national and international issues.

Library of Congress Cataloging-in-Publication Data

Main entry under title:

Are world population trends a problem?

    Papers presented at an AEI conference held in
Washington, D.C. in Dec. 1984.
    Bibliogaphy: p.
    1. Demography--Congresses. 2. Population--
Congresses. 3. Population policy--Congresses.
I. Wattenberg, Ben J. II. Zinsmeister, Karl.
III. American Enterprise Institute for Public Policy
Research.
HB849.A75 1985   304.6   85-11099
ISBn 0-8447-1374-0

ISBN 0-8447-1374-0

Printed in the United States of America

Cover photograph courtesy of the World Bank.

Contents

Foreword

"Are world population trends a problem?" That simple question might not even have been asked a few years ago.

From the publication of Paul Ehrlich's *The Population Bomb* in 1968 right up into the later 1970s, there existed widespread belief that world population trends were a problem, and a big one. The links between population growth and environmental and economic conditions were widely thought to be negative. The energy shocks of the 1970s inspired much speculation on possible limits to human expansion and put pressure on living standards in both developed and underdeveloped countries. For the first time, demographic and environmental questions took on pressing interest for the general media, political leaders, and the public at large.

Population is now a front-burner issue. Polls consistently show it ranking as one of the public's foremost international concerns. With the importance of the debate established, the arguments about population are maturing, and the field bubbles with new energy of contention. In the past ten years, research has begun to give us some answers to age-old population-growth questions: Where are the problems? Are there benefits? What is the best response?

It has become clear that population debates —and the larger ecology and economic develop-ment debates that subsume them—are undergoing crucial shifts. And so, in December of 1984 AEI organized a forum on the subject at the institute's annual Public Policy Week. Papers were commissioned from three leading international population experts, and a wide cross section of distinguished commentators was invited to discuss the major issues.

This volume includes an edited transcript of that conference, a historical and intellectual introduction to the subject by Ben Wattenberg and Karl Zinsmeister, and statistical and bibliographical appendixes. Taken as a whole, these materials serve as a convenient distillation of the debate among the best minds in the field of world population and a road sign to possible developments ahead.

We plan to continue and expand our research in these areas at AEI. In fact, we envision this book as the first product of what we hope will become a major new center, established to investigate problems and public policy responses in the areas of population, resources, environment, and Third World development.

WILLIAM J. BAROODY, JR.
President
American Enterprise Institute

v

Introduction:
The Argument about
"Supply-Side Demographics"

BEN WATTENBERG AND KARL ZINSMEISTER

SHORTLY after the conclusion of the World Population Conference held by the U.N. in Mexico City last year, the editor of a leading American magazine called our office.

"What's going on?" he asked. "Until recently all I ever heard about was 'the population bomb,' 'the population crisis,' and 'the population explosion.' But now I hear some experts saying there's no bomb, no explosion, no crisis. Something has happened."

Indeed, something important has happened in the field of population. There is an argument going on. And even people who still believe in the bomb-explosion-crisis scenario feel the ground shifting beneath their feet.

In a major article in *Foreign Affairs* in Summer of 1984, Robert McNamara, a firm believer in the crisis view, wrote, "Many . . . believe that the world in general and most countries in particular no longer face serious population problems." He added, "Editorial writers and commentators in the mass media have been quick . . . to take up this theme, announcing the end of the population explosion or declaring rapid population growth to be 'another non-crisis.'" McNamara's article, of course, argues that "such a view is totally in error."

The dispute is an important one—more than a clash among experts, a confrontation between editorialists, or an academic argument.

Population levels spring from the most intimate human behavior—decisions about family size, sexual practice, household economics, and so forth. Population affects, or is alleged to affect, many other important and sensitive issues that are the daily stuff of headlines: resource availability, international migration, energy consumption, pollution, national income, and military security. There is a religious component to the argument. And lurking in the background, but clearly present in some aspects of the population control debate, are racial fears. The stakes of the dispute are high.

What, then, has changed in the Great People Debate?

Two things. New facts. And new theorists, promulgating theories both new and old with vigor and originality.

New Facts

The most important new aspect of the old debate has been the dramatic change in the demographic situation. As recently as 1970, women in the less-developed world (as defined by the U.N.) were bearing a lifetime average of 6.1 children. Today, it is 4.1 children. When you consider that eventually 2.1 children would produce stable populations in the Less-Developed Countries

1

(simple replacement of the mother and father with a factor for childhood mortality), it can be seen that *in 15 years, the less-developed world moved more than halfway toward a rate that yields "zero population growth."*

Now, it can properly be pointed out that all the LDCs did not share equally in this reduction. Fertility in Asia dropped very rapidly, while in parts of Africa it stayed high.

But, after all, it was in Asia (with 2.7 billion people, more than half the world's total) that the population problem was supposed to be worst. Africa, the partial exception to the worldwide downward trend, is still regarded by many as a relatively sparsely populated continent with 500 million total inhabitants and low overall density even excluding desert areas. So: to the extent that high fertility is a global problem, the global numbers are down sharply.

Although many demographers believe that the "Total Fertility Rates" cited above are the best single indicators of reproductive behavior, they are measures that population explosionists rarely use. Their preferred measure is simple "Annual Population Growth," expressed as either an absolute number or a rate. Even here there has been considerable reduction: from 2.1 percent more people every year in 1970 to less than 1.7 percent today.[1] But, the explosionists point out, because of our larger base, even at the lower rate, record numbers of new people are being added to the world every year—82 million last year.

There is a logic to their case. It is terribly easy, in the statistical field, to get so caught up in abstractions like percentages and growth rates that one loses track of the brute facts. And 82 million new people every year is a brute fact.

Just the same, brute facts too can be misleading. Imagine a very large pendulum. As two observers watch, it is drawn back and allowed to swing one arc. As the pendulum approaches the end of that arc, the observers describe what they see.

"The pendulum is *ten* feet from its center point," notes the first observer, "further than it's been at any time on its arc!"

"Yes," replies the second observer. "But it's never been moving more slowly. It won't go much further."

Now, it will undoubtedly be several more decades before the pendulum of world population growth reaches its stopping point. But it is also true that it is moving more slowly now than at any time since World War II. And in some very important countries it has already reversed itself.

Negative Population Growth

The fallacy of relying exclusively on population growth rates is perhaps best illustrated among the rich, industrialized nations. For instance, the European countries, taken as a whole, are currently growing at about .3 percent a year, over 8 million people in the last five years. That does not sound like a problem. But it is.

The "Total Fertility Rate" for Europeans is about 1.8 lifetime children per woman (roughly the same as in the U.S.). That means the Europeans are not even replacing themselves. That means that, barring massive immigration or an increase in the birth rate (neither of which the Europeans have shown themselves willing to accept), those countries will not only lose population as soon as the current generation starts to pass from the scene, but will lose population with gathering speed.

At current rates, by the time a baby born today in West Germany reaches age 50, he will live in a nation in sharp decline: the population reduced by 16 million, with bigger losses on the way, *half* the population over 50, with the likelihood of massive shortages of workers, soldiers, and people to pay for the tremendous social security obligations. There will be empty houses, empty schools, shrinking markets for manufacturers. The developed, industrial democratic nations will comprise an ever-declining share of the world's peoples. And even if today's baby and his age-mates try to turn things around by having an extra child, it will not be easy. There will be too few of them of childbearing age.[2]

This is not a scenario. This is what will happen unless something changes. In fact, it has already begun. Last year, five European countries actually lost population. West Germany's Total Fertility Rate is now down to 1.3 children per woman. (Remember it takes over two for replacement.) Theirs is the lowest case at present, but below-replacement rates are now the norm throughout the industrial world. This "birth dearth" portending a population collapse is very real, but it does not (yet) show up in a quick glance at the "Growth Rates" favored by explosionists.

Theorists

So: the path toward "Zero Population Growth" and "Negative Population Growth" already obtains in the developed world. And in the less-developed world, the issue is less *if* population stability will be achieved than *when*.

The important question then becomes, "Is there an *optimum* amount of population?" This much? A little more? A little less? At what level do we want to stabilize?

Through most of the 1970s, there would have been little ambivalence about that important question. The explosionists insisted, less was more. After all, more people means more mouths to feed, more feet to shoe, more schools to build, more resources burned up, more consumption. More people, in short, meant more trouble. Many theorists viewed people as a kind of pollution.

But, recently, another view of the relationship between population growth and economic growth has gained credence. Every baby, the demurrers point out, comes equipped with two hands and a brain as well as a mouth. People not only consume, they produce— food, capital, even resources. (More properly, they produce the ideas which transform the useless resource into the useful resource.) The individuals prominently associated with this new theorizing include Simon Kuznets, P. T. Bauer, Colin Clark, Julian Simon, Ester Boserup, and others. (In deference to the idea of full disclosure, it should be mentioned that Mr. Wattenberg has been associated with this view over the years.) This is a production-ethic view of population. It might be called a "supply-side demography." Population growth need not be bad; in some cases, it may even be good (as for instance in large stretches of Africa, where the sparseness of population prevents the erection of modern communications and transportation infrastructure). Most commonly, it is maintained, population growth is economically neutral. Indeed, data show economic growth or economic decline proceeding without pattern at almost every level of fertility, from low to high.

The Conference

It was against this contentious backdrop, freshly colored by the publicity surrounding the U.N.'s Mexico City population meeting in August of 1984, that AEI organized the conference whose proceedings comprise this volume.

Three papers were commissioned. The first of these was by *Samuel Preston,* the director of the Population Studies Center at the University of Pennsylvania, and, at the time, President of the Population Association of America.

Referring to the conclusions of a report he has prepared for the National Academy of Sciences, Preston states that ". . . rapid population growth in most times and places is a relatively minor factor in reducing per capita income and other indicators of welfare." Preston argues, though, that while it is minor in importance, population may be easier and cheaper to manipulate than other influences on development, and that family planning is therefore a cost-effective strategy. He maintains that family-planning programs, by making information and services available, simply "increase the private well-being of couples who use [them] and leave unaffected the welfare of those who do not. In other words, they increase private welfare at a public cost." Of course, this enhanced private welfare argument depends critically upon governments allowing couples to make reproductive decisions themselves, voluntarily.

The second paper was presented by *Rafael Salas,* director of the U.N. Fund for Population Activities, who has headed the United Nations' family-planning effort since its inception. Mr. Salas, Secretary-General of the 1984 World Population Conference (Mexico City), summarizes the recommendations of that decennial gathering. He states that U.N. population programs are built upon a respect for national sovereignty and the principles of the Universal Declaration of Human Rights. The U.N., he points out, does not take specific positions on population policy, but rather reflects, and assists, the demographic choices of the U.N.'s member countries. However, says Mr. Salas, national population policies must also be compatible with what he calls "global realities."

The third paper is by *Peter Bauer* of the London School of Economics. He argues that it is largely at the urging of Westerners that Third World nations have undertaken population-control programs, and that those programs are generally founded on false premises. Both economic history and contemporary developments, states Lord Bauer, conclusively refute the notion that rapid population increases are deleterious to economic well-being. He reviews and attempts to refute the familiar claims of land shortage, resource depletion, capital dilution, job shortages, famine, high social service expeditures, and per capita income reduction. He then argues that most parents in the Third World want the children they have, for a variety of psychic and economic reasons.

Bauer maintains that the clearest inducement to restriction of family size among peoples in LDC's is Westernization, through trade and contact with international commercial enterprises, as well as education, exposure to mass media, travel, and other cultural contacts. Fertility levels, he says, will decline apace with cultural "modernization." In the meantime, Lord Bauer argues, decisions about fertility must be left to individual families. There is great danger, he says, that once a central government begins to prescribe population-level goals, socially disruptive propagandizing and social and economic pressure may follow. This is especially true in Third World nations where most economic and political rights and privileges are officially disbursed.

Four distinguished commentators then deliver brief reactions to the papers. *Allen Kelley* of Duke University, whose academic specialization is precisely the relationship of population and economics, applauds the revisionist thinking. He says it "places population in its proper perspective. Population is neither villain nor hero in the economic development story. It's instead an important actor in a complex plot."

Julian Simon of the University of Maryland points out that there is little or no evidence in the scientific literature demonstrating a long-run negative relationship between population growth and economic growth, or resource availability, educational accomplishment, and so forth.

Nancy Birdsall of the World Bank says that though much of the rhetoric about population growth has been exaggerated, it is nonetheless a problem which deserves more attention than the relatively small amount of money currently devoted to it by the international community.

James Schall of Georgetown University asks that we keep in mind that "population" is but an undifferentiated abstraction for "people," and that ultimately any population policy must be founded upon a respect for individual persons, an understanding of man's inherent dignity, and

support for the transmission of human life on earth.

A lively and sometimes argumentative discussion follows. Werner Fornos of the Population Institute is prominent in suggesting that a world growing by 83 million people a year portends a grave threat to global stability, the quality of life, and resource and environmental protection.

In general, however, there was loose agreement that the conclusions of the 1970s, with their emphasis on "final limits" and imminent danger, have passed from the scene, and thankfully so. The importance of population was not unduly discounted, but it was made clear that population should not be made a crutch for the social and economic failures of governments. Third World leaders and Western aid-givers, it was argued, must acknowledge that the immediate responsibility for alleviating human suffering and misery properly lies in the area of economic organization.

Mexico City

That was one of the major points of the American delegation at the Mexico City Conference. Economic development, said the U.S. policy, deserved equal emphasis with family planning for two reasons. First, it is often the equivalent of a powerful contraceptive itself. Numerous studies show that improvements in income, education, and health, and the changes in living conditions and cultural mores which economic development brings, all act powerfully to suppress fertility.

This is the position Indira Gandhi came around to in recent years. In 1984 Mrs. Gandhi stated:

> The very best way of inducing people to have smaller families is more development. Where we have highly industrialized areas or much better education or even much better agriculture, we find automatically families tend to grow smaller.

With this in mind, it was the American position in Mexico that, all things considered, "a more-free economy is more efficient than a less-free economy." This was not a rigid endorsement of *laissez-faire* economics, but merely a recognition—and one apparently shared even by the Chinese, Hungarians, and other Eastern bloc countries—that attaining vigorous economic performance may require encouragement of entrepreneurial incentives, and decentralization.

The other intervention of the American delegation was a plank pointing out that contrary to the popular conventional wisdom, life quality has been improving in the developing world over the last several decades. It was pointed out that the infant mortality rate in LDCs was down 67 percent since 1955, life expectancy at birth was up 16 years over the same period. And no wonder: the number of physicians per unit of population more than doubled from 1960 to 1980. Over the same period, calorie supply *per capita* increased from 87 percent of daily requirements to 97 percent. Income per person doubled in constant dollars. Adult literacy rates went from one-quarter to one-half, as primary, secondary, and higher education enrollment rates jumped. All this according to U.N. and World Bank data. Recognizing that enormous progress had already occurred was, in the view of the U.S. delegation, a prerequisite to further international aid efforts. We succeed; therefore, we can continue to succeed.

Goals

It is interesting that in both the conclave of nations in Mexico City and the conclave of scholars at AEI, despite much divergent analysis, the contending parties expressed considerable agreement on *goals*. Virtually all sides agreed that fertility rates should—and would—continue to come down. There was general support for voluntary family-planning programs—and only voluntary family-planning programs. The nut of the argument was over how insistently family planning should be promoted, whether it should be organized by private, governmental, or voluntary organizations, and what its relative effectiveness is vis-à-vis other fertility suppressants, like Westernization or economic development.[3]

To us at least, it appears that family-planning programs are surely useful tools, but cannot accomplish the job by themselves. For one example of why this is the case, consider the following. Surveys show that throughout the less developed world, when women are asked what number of children they consider *ideal*, what number they would *like* to have in their lifetime, how many they *desire*, the answer averages about four. In Mexico, for instance, it is 4.5 children per woman. This is not terribly surprising. After all, most people in the Third World still live in rural settings—in villages, where practices tend to be traditional, and values change slowly.[4] Most families in Third World nations still *want* relatively large families.

Think what that implies for family planners. Even if—miraculously—every single sexually active Mexican man and woman could be equipped tomorrow with a 100-percent-effective contraceptive, the Mexican population would still approximately double with each generation.

And the same thing holds true elsewhere in the developing world. The World Fertility Survey canvassed ten nations in Africa. It showed African women want families even *larger* than the current already high average of over six children.

It is clear, then, that social attitudes, birth desires and expectations, must be transformed before population stability can be reached. That requires education, income security, improved communications, health, perhaps urbanization. In short: modernization, Westernization, economic development.[5] It would not be correct to say that high world fertility is just a result of unmet demand for modern contraception.

Beyond deferring to socioeconomic development where appropriate, there are things that can be done to make sure family-planning efforts remain both voluntary and humane. The first is simply to remember that *people*—not birth quotas, or fertility timetables or growth rates—are the point. And to recognize that people are generally pretty good at recognizing what is in their own best interests, and at conforming their behavior to those requirements.

The second trick is to recognize that, in our world of increasingly centralized power, there is simply too much temptation for planners to start wielding financial carrots and police sticks against individual families in this most sensitive area. Clearly it is important that family planners avoid, in their zeal, extending tacit acceptance (as some have done, scandalously) to the type of brutally coercive policies now being pursued in China.[6]

The most prominent result of AEI's conference was to reinforce the axiom that ideas have consequences. If we get away from the belief that population growth is a catastrophic, geometric, uncontrollable horror, we are less likely to stumble into dangerous overreactions. Instead we can look at real problems—old and new—and considerable—if incomplete—success, and then begin to focus on real solutions. One sensed a new maturity, confidence, and balance, a steelier eye, in the thinking going on at this conference. Perhaps we are entering a new era.

Notes

1. 2.4 percent to 2.0 percent in the LDCs. Both rates would have fallen even faster but for the tremendous—almost miraculous—reductions in death rates around the world.

2. Based on a projection assuming constant fertility done by the statistical branch of the World Bank, total population for the Federal Republic of Germany would fall from 62 million today to 46 million 50 years from now—a decline of 26 percent, with an even sharper decline set in motion.

3. An additional source of controversy, not treated here because it does not bear on the economic-development effects of population, was the U.S. Administration's decision to end funding for private agencies which promoted abortion internationally.

4. All of which makes the progress of the 1970s seem even more remarkable.

5. Among other institutions, international corporations—the *bêtes noires* of liberals and dependency theorists —have probably had a very salutary effect in this area, and will continue to do so where they are allowed to operate.

6. In 1983, well after its abuses were documented, the U.N. co-awarded its first medal for family-planning achievement to Qian Xinzhong, head of the Chinese program. For detailed information on current Chinese practice, see *The Washington Post* series, "One Couple—One Child," January 6, 7, 8, 1985; or *Broken Earth* by Steven Mosher, 1983.

Are World Population Trends a Problem?

AEI Conference, December 5, 1984

PARTICIPANTS

Lord P. T. Bauer, London School of Economics
Sam Baum, U.S. Bureau of the Census
Nancy Birdsall, World Bank
Nick Eberstadt, Harvard University
Tom Espenshade, Urban Institute
Werner Fornos, Population Institute
Ed Hullander, U.S. Agency for International
Development
D. Gale Johnson, University of Chicago
Allen Kelley, Duke University
Deepak Lal, World Bank
Ambassador Clare Boothe Luce
Tom Merrick, Population Reference Bureau
Samuel Preston, University of Pennsylvania
Rafael Salas, United Nations Fund for Population
Activities
Father James Schall, Georgetown University
Julian Simon, University of Maryland
Ben Wattenberg, American Enterprise Institute
Karl Zinsmeister, American Enterprise Institute

Samuel Preston

Director, Population Study Center
University of Pennsylvania
1984 President, Population Association of America

I think it is useful to begin by recognizing that any social unit within which reproduction is occurring is faced with a population problem. The problem is one of choosing the proper balance between the amount of resources available and the number of people who have claims on those resources). This problem is unlike any other that the unit would face, because the outcome determines the number of feeling, thinking, producing, and reproducing human beings. How one values the welfare of people who may never be born clearly affects one's solution to this problem.

In the vast majority of societies, the basic right to make the reproductive decision is ceded to individual families. This concession reflects several notions, especially the belief that choosing one's family size is a basic human right, and the belief that families are the best judges of their own circumstances and able to make rational decisions.

But most societies also provide an array of incentives and disincentives to child-bearing. Many of these are adopted without regard to their reproductive consequences. Increasingly, however, these consequences are direct objects of policy.

The two largest countries in the world have in the past decade undertaken to reduce their rates of population growth in ways that directly violate family sovereignty in reproductive decisions. India quickly abandoned its experiment in forced sterilization in response to a public outcry, but China is pushing resolutely ahead with its sanctions against large families.

The logic of government intervention in couples' reproductive lives rests on two grounds. First, that the sum of private decisions results in an outcome that is socially undesirable. In effect, the argument goes, couples are not taking account of the impact of their private decisions on the welfare of others.

The so-called externalities from having a child are believed to be positive in Europe, where many countries have decided to stimulate childbearing through financial incentives. France has been concerned for a century that its national power is being demographically eroded, and other countries are trying to offset the rapid aging of their populations and the enormous burden that this is placing on social security systems.

But in developing countries, of course, the externalities are widely believed to be negative.

The second justification for government involvement in reproduction is that governments can supply information and services bearing on the reproductive process more efficiently and more cheaply than can the private sector. Some of these services are fertility-enhancing, but the most important are fertility-reducing. Very large investments are required in order for the private sector to undertake these activities, and not all of the benefits to the consumer can be captured by the price mechanism. Who is going to make a profit, for example, by delivering the rhythm method?

The information supplied need not be limited to contraceptive methods, but can include

---

". . . there is a rationale for most existing national and international efforts in [the family planning] area that does not require resort to doomsday rhetoric. This [is] important since so much of the rhetoric is simple-minded and incorrect, casually attributing any human problem to there being too many humans."

---

evidence on the health and economic consequences of alternate family sizes. So there is a logical case here for government intervention. Many precedents for these activities exist in such areas as agricultural extension programs, public health programs, and even the postal service.

This second ground, I think, is a sufficient justification for government sponsorship of family planning programs, which is the form assumed by the bulk of population program assistance in developing countries. Such programs simply make information and contraceptive services available. They increase the private well-being of couples who use their services and leave unaffected the welfare of those who do not. In other words, they increase private welfare at a public cost. If we accept this second justification, as I do, then there are only two grounds for governments not being involved in family planning programs—first, that such programs are cost-ineffective, not worth the money spent. That conclusion may, in fact, appear to have been justified a decade ago. But recently, there have been very large fertility declines in many developing countries, declines that seem to be associated with intensified family planning programs; in Mexico, Indonesia, Thailand, Colombia, for example.

The implication of this success, I think, is that family planning programs in many settings have, in fact, increased welfare by reducing the gap between desired numbers of children and the actual number of children. I suspect that this increment in welfare has been achieved in most places at a moderate and justifiable cost, although the matter of cost needs, I think, far more attention than it has received.

A second possible rationale for withholding family planning services is that the positive externalities of population growth far outweigh the private benefits of family planning programs. There are only a few areas of the world where I believe that one could begin to make this argument plausible.

In Central Africa, especially Zaire, and in the Amazon Basin, the predominant agricultural technique is slash and burn, and the soil can support considerable intensification of agricultural practice. The areas are very sparsely populated relative to resources, and it is possible that denser populations would enjoy higher per capita incomes, better government services, and better integration into national and international economies.

Apart from these areas, I think it would be very hard to make the case that family planning programs do more harm than good.

I conclude that the grounds for withholding family planning services are generally very weak. Note that this conclusion is reached without invoking the catalogue of horrors that many attribute to rapid population growth. It seems to me important to recognize that there is a rationale for most existing national and international efforts in this area that does not require resort to

---

". . . rapid population growth in most times and places is a relatively minor factor in reducing per capita income and other measures of welfare."

---

doomsday rhetoric. This dissociation is particularly important since so much of the rhetoric is simple-minded and incorrect, casually attributing any human problem to there being too many humans. If and when the balloon bursts, I think it would be a pity if family planning programs were an automatic victim.

Many responsible people, of course, believe that family planning programs are not enough; they serve merely to reduce the gap between private benefits and costs of children, and except for the relatively minor tax and subsidies that are entailed, don't appropriately take into account the negative externalities of population growth. This view requires some kind of an assessment of the importance of these externalities, which is obviously a massive task. I can only here state some tentative conclusions that I have reached in helping prepare a report for the National Academy of Sciences and that I believe to be shared by a number of other people including Allen Kelley, Simon Kuznets, Timothy King, and the World Bank, in the substantive sections of the 1984 World Development Report.

The conclusion is that rapid population growth in most times and places is a relatively minor factor in reducing per capita income and other measures of welfare.

If we could conduct a thought experiment in which we transfer conditions of developed countries one at a time into developing countries and could evaluate their impact on well-being, I daresay that the improvement from changing all demographic circumstances—size, density, population growth rate, and age structure—would rank far down the list. The greatest gains would occur from the transfer of productive technique; of social, political and legal institutions; of the knowl-

> "If we could conduct a thought experiment in which we transfer conditions of developed countries one at a time into developing countries . . . I daresay that the improvement from changing all demographic circumstances . . . would rank far down the list."

edge embodied in human beings; of entrepreneurship and administrative ability, and of the stock of physical capital.

Of course, demographic factors affect these other items, just as the other items affect populations. But the accumulation of evidence suggests that these effects are weak. Surely, they are not strong enough to dominate statistical associations between national population growth rates and growth rates of income per capita, which look about as random and unstructured as any relation in the social sciences.

The fact that population growth may be a minor factor in the international income distribution by this standard does not, of course, mean that social intervention to alter rates of growth may not be one of the most cost-effective strategies available. Automobile accidents, for example, are a minor cause of death in the United States, but cost-benefit analysis of health interventions repeatedly shows that prevention of automobile accidents has the highest payoff per health dollar spent.

More intensive investigation of particular features of these relations suggests a highly varied pattern of effects of population growth on elements that contribute to economic production. The first relationship to draw attention was that between population and land. Malthus argued that beyond a certain point, added numbers would produce diminishing returns to the fixed supply of land. Because added workers would have less land to work with on average, per capita output would fall.

Although it is now common to assert that Malthus was wrong—that historically, added numbers have been accompanied by greatly expanded production per capita—it is safe to say that the basic Malthusian notions still dominate most of our thinking about population/economic relations. The concept of land, of course, has been expanded to include natural resources of many types.

Malthus was not wrong about diminishing returns. He simply underestimated the capacity of technical change and man-made factors of production to offset the effects of reductions in per capita availability of natural resources. We do live in a world of diminishing returns, as is evident, for example, in the reduced marginal gains in yields from increments in fertilizer use.

In dealing with the issue of natural resources, it is important, I think, to distinguish renewable resources such as land, forests, air and water from the largely nonrenewable resources such as minerals and most forms of energy.

We are eventually going to run out of those resources whose deposits are strictly limited. It is

> "Malthus was not wrong about diminishing returns. He simply underestimated the capacity of technical change and man-made factors of production to offset the effects of reductions in per capita availability of natural resources."

reasonable to suppose that we will run out of them sooner in a situation where populations are growing faster. However, there is little cause for alarm in this proposition if our concern is with people rather than with time itself. If only 100 billion people can enjoy some fixed resource at a particular standard of use, I see no particular reason why we should care how those people are distributed through time. We have to hope that the price mechanism and administrative organs operate efficiently to allocate those resources over people and to stimulate the search for substitutes, for new technologies and for conservation measures. If they don't, we face the same set of problems with a rapidly or slowly growing population. Yes, we could postpone a crisis with slower growth, but we are not necessarily going to make any people better off by doing so.[1]

The case for renewable resources, I think, is different. First of all, a larger steady-state population will certainly have fewer of these resources per capita than a smaller population. This is likely not only to reduce income, but also to worsen income disparities by increasing the payments to resource owners relative to the payments to labor.

Second, if the price mechanism is not working efficiently to allocate those resources over time, then we face the possibility that we could be doing serious and perhaps permanent damage to our resource base. In areas of nomadism, where shifting cultivation is used, where forests can be freely exploited for firewood, where resources are held in common, rapid population growth can intensify a downward spiral of resource resiliency.

Other serious charges have been levelled at population growth. One is that it leads to a reduced volume of physical capital for workers, and hence, to lowered productivity. It was this claim that undergirded a major expansion of American efforts in the area of population assistance in the 1960s. The potential relations here are exceedingly complex. While it is likely that more children in the family put added pressure on consumption and reduce investable resources, the effect is frequently mitigated by the tendency for an added child to induce greater family work effort. Furthermore, when population increases relative to capital in the short term, it can increase the returns to capital and hence provide more in-

come for, and more savings in, the families that own substantial capital and that provide for the bulk of household savings. Businesses can foresee a more rapid expansion in the number of future consumers and undertake new investments. So can governments.

As economists have come to recognize the limited role of physical capital per worker as a source of economic growth and have defined an expanded role for technique and for human capital, attention has shifted to the effect of population growth on these variables. Here, there is even less evidence, I think, than in the case of physical capital. It is true that it will be more expensive for a government to educate the same fraction of a nation's youth when populations are growing more rapidly. But if it succeeds in educating the same fraction despite more rapid growth, then the educational qualifications of the labor force will increase more rapidly than when growth is slower. That is, more rapid growth simply means more rapid turnover in the labor force and provides the opportunity for a faster upgrading of labor force quality, even while at the same time it might be reducing the resources available for such an upgrading. The net effect of population growth on human capital formation is to me unclear, and seems to depend critically upon how governments respond to more rapid population growth.

The strongest pro-growth argument makes its appearance in this area of technical change. Many have suggested that more rapid population growth will speed the pace of technical innovations, in large measure because there will be more innovators in a larger population. I think that it is reasonable to consider the volume of technical innovation to be, in fact, a direct function of population size, once the many other and more important determinants of technical innovations are controlled. But this argument, I think, suffers from the same time fallacy as the argument on the other side about fixed resources. If we grant the assumption that more people mean more innovations, we will reach a particular stage of technique at an earlier time when populations grow faster. But we will reach that stage after approximately the same number of people have lived. The ten billion and first person to live will have access to the same innovations introduced by the first ten billion, regardless of when he or she is born. Unless we care

---

1. Here I am making the assumption that technical progress in resource utilization is not "exogenous" to populations but is a direct function of supply and demand conditions in markets for the resources which are in turn a function of population size.

about the welfare of time itself, faster population growth buys us nothing here.

We know, I think, very little about many of the effects of population growth on physical and human capital formation. Yet many of the present population control efforts are partially justified by the presumed negative effects of population growth that work through these elements.

The U.S. Agency for International Development has been particularly averse to sponsoring research in these areas, appearing to consider the case closed. In one sense, they are right. I have tried to argue that a strong case for family planning programs can be made without resort to ar-

---

"... there is no doubt that U.S. support for population control measures is profiting from perceptions of a crisis. But this can do damage...."

---

guments about the negative effects of population growth. And there is no doubt that U.S. support for population control measures is profiting from perceptions of a crisis.

But this can do damage, as illustrated by the go-slow attitude that the U.S. and some other developed countries have adopted in the area of international health. James Grant, Director of UNICEF, says that the most common objection he hears to UNICEF's proposals for major new efforts in world health is that such efforts will accentuate the population problem. It is hard for me to imagine a more grotesque perversion of priorities. We withhold measures that can save lives and reduce sickness in order to avoid the consequences of rapid population growth. But what could be a worse outcome of such growth than unnecessary death and disease?

I think it is important that funding for population programs, like other programs, be put on solid ground. In my view, a good case can be made for family planning programs nearly everywhere, and a reasonable case for additional incentive-type measures where renewable resources are being damaged by rapid population growth. To go beyond these statements would take us into some very shaky territory.

Rafael M. Salas

*Executive Director, United Nations
Fund for Population Activities*

I would like to begin by stating and reporting to you as Secretary-General of the 1984 World Population Conference in Mexico City. This is the second time the world has called a conference on population. The first was in 1974, when 136 states came together to agree by consensus on the World Population Plan of Action. And again, ten years after, 146 states this time adhered to the consensus.

Now, there were 88 recommendations in the Mexico Conference, and these range through all the fields of population. I want to emphasize at the outset that the concern of countries is not just with growth, although it is quite important for many of them, but includes many other aspects which I will explain in brief later.

Now, in looking at these recommendations and the World Population Plan of Action, we must bear three principles very clearly in mind. The first is that these recommendations on population are always integrated in the minds of the countries with economic development and economic planning. There is in almost every developing country a unit in charge of linking population with the development process, usually in the ministries of planning or in the ministries of health.

The second principle is that national sovereignty is respected in all these population policies. There are, in fact, as many as 159 views of population, as there are countries. The United Nations itself does not prescribe any approach to population. Support is given to all countries—Mongolia, which has a pro-natalist policy, as well as China and India, who have policies for controlling fertility. Other countries that do not pay at-

> **"The United Nations itself does not prescribe any approach to population. Support is given to all countries."**

tention either to growth or family planning are assisted, like the countries of the Sahel, Mauritania and others, that are interested in migratory movements or interested in getting basic data for economic planning.

The third principle is that individuals must have the freedom of choice in the number and spacing of their children. No UN program really can be supported that violates this principle.

Before I go to discussion of the conference recommendations, I would like to give you an insight of what has occurred in the last ten years in the population field.

First is the decline in global fertility rates; second, the increasing importance of developing countries in world population trends; third, the expansion in global awareness and understanding of population issues. And here, I must state categorically that there is no developing country that does not have a population policy or program. The United Nations Fund for Population

Activities has funded, in the course of 15 years, 145 developing countries and territories, and in all of these, we have population projects. Now, population policy should not be understood as only limiting fertility. As I have already said, several countries—Gabon, Central African Republic, others—are for the increase of fertility. That is population policy. Or take the case of Bolivia. It is interested in transferring population from the Andes to the lower parts of the country. That is a population policy. In the United Nations system, population programs range from basic data collection—we have supported 22 African countries south of the Sahara to conduct their first censuses—to projects on urbanization and migration, communication and education, and of course, family planning.

"Nearly 90 percent of the annual increase in world population is contributed by the developing countries."

Let us go to some population data. Developed countries as a group are presently experiencing very low rates of population growth of about 0.64 percent annually. Among developing regions, the decline was most significant in Asia, dropping from 2.5 to 1.7 percent over the last decade, largely the result of rapid reduction in China's growth rate. The Latin American region experienced a modest reduction from 2.6 to 2.3 percent. By contrast, the African region has shown a rising trend, from 2.6 to 3.0 percent.

Nearly 90 percent of the annual increase in world population is contributed by the developing countries; the annual rate of population growth in developing countries is at least three times as large as in the developed countries. Total fertility is twice as high as in developed countries. The average number of desired children, though declining on the whole, still ranges between 3.0 and 8.6 in developing countries. The average life expectancy at birth in developing countries, though it has much improved, is still lagging at 56.6 years as compared to 73 years for developed countries. Finally, the phenomenon of urbanization and particularly metropolitan growth has been most pronounced in the developing countries. There are expected to be about 60 cities with populations of 4 million or more by the year 2000.

Perceptions and policies in developing countries have responded to these demographic changes. According to the assessment of 129 developing countries undertaken by the UN, almost 80 percent of the total population of the developing world, in 62 countries, live under governments which consider national levels of fertility too high. Fewer than 2 percent live in 12 countries which would like their fertility rates increased. The remaining 55 countries, with 18 percent of the population, consider fertility satisfactory or have other priorities. As I mentioned, it could be urbanization, migration, and others. Access to modern methods of family planning is officially restricted in only six countries. In 97, there is some form of government support to family planning activities. In areas other than fertility, 98 governments consider mortality too high, while population distribution patterns are considered unsatisfactory by 75 countries.

The UN's response to this recognition by the international community of the importance of population has been to package various programs, depending on the policy of the countries themselves. So you will usually find in the programs that are supported by the UN, an element on communication and education, basic data collection, family planning, population dynamics, policy formulation and implementation, and some special programs, like those for women, youth, or the aged, and multi-sector activities for regional or global groupings of countries.

These principles confirm the giving of assistance for population, respect for national sovereignty, neutrality in judgment, effectiveness and flexibility in the approach to these population problems.

I would like now to go to the main provisions of the recommendations of Mexico. The first stresses the most important principle, that population programs are part of the socio-economic development programs of countries; second, there is a very extensive provision on the role and status of women; third, governments are urged to adopt population policies and social and development policies which are mutually reinforcing with the reaffirmation of the first. Fourth, countries which consider that their population growth rates hinder the attainment of national goals were invited to consider relevant demographic policies. The Plan itself and the 88 recommendations do not set targets. It depends on the countries. Fifth is the strong emphasis on morbidity and mortality, particularly infant mortality and maternal morbidity and mortality. Sixth, reproduction and the family—it was not the intention of the Conference to set targets for family size or birth rates. Instead, countries which have adopted or intend to adopt national fertility goals were called upon to translate them into specific, clearly-understood policies and operational steps.

Now, there are important provisions in the Mexico City Plan which were not in the Bucharest Plan ten years ago. It should be noted that natural family planning was mentioned in these 88 recommendations, and that the role of the family was emphasized. And what is more, as part of the U.S. intervention it was stated explicitly that abortion is not to be promoted as a means of family planning.

There is in the 1984 Plan a promotion of knowledge—and I must say that among the international conferences sponsored by the UN, this is unique in the sense of the very large number of provisions for scientifically basing policies and studies on increased knowledge—and therefore, very strong provisions for research and applications of this research.

Now, let me conclude this presentation by saying what it is, really, that we are aiming at in all these population activities. First of all, the World Population Plan of Action and the 88 recommendations are really only guidelines for countries to follow. It is left to the countries to decide what particular population policy or program they wish to have.

Recognition of the time element is essential. Population policies and programs vary in the periods allowed for accomplishing their ends.

> **"Given the very long-term nature of population processing, long-term goals need to be harmonized with varied short-term objectives. It is also important that national population policy be compatible with global realities."**

Given the very long-term nature of population processing, long-term goals need to be harmo-

nized with varied short-term objectives. It is also important that national population policy be compatible with global realities.

Policy makers, including those of you who are here, are constantly reminded that population policies are subject to change. Human knowledge becomes deeper and more extensive, and perceptions of the impact of population on our existence are changed as a result.

In order to permit the international community to assess these changes, I myself proposed at the conclusion of the Mexico meeting that a population conference be convened every ten years, the next in 1994, to assess these changes.

The World Population Plan of Action states that population policies should respect human life and aim to improve the levels of living and the quality of life of all people in all countries. Population policies exist for the preservation of human life and for a more satisfying future for the developing countries in particular. They exist to help bring about a global society that is secure and viable, free from capricious inequalities of development and threats of environmental degradation, a society in which individuals can develop their

> **"Internationally accepted [population] policies can achieve their purpose without violating either the sovereignty of nations or the dignity and freedom of the human person."**

full potential. One of the essential elements of population policy is therefore to give all people the education which will enable them to assess their own situation, as well as the knowledge, the means and the motivation to make fully informed and responsible choices on the number and spacing of their children.

Internationally accepted policies can achieve their purpose without violating either the sovereignty of nations or the dignity and freedom of the human person. To do so will require sustained attention by governments and by individuals to the importance of population. From the evidence of the Conference, the international community is prepared to make that commitment.

Lord P. T. Bauer

London School of Economics

POPULATION pressure and growth are widely regarded as prime causes of Third World poverty and prime obstacles to development. In Mr. McNamara's colourful words: "To put it simply: The greatest single obstacle to the economic and social advancement of the majority of peoples in the underdeveloped world is rampant population growth . . . the threat of unmanageable population pressures is very much like the threat of nuclear war. . . . Both threats can and will have catastrophic consequences unless they are dealt with rapidly and rationally."[1]

According to these ideas Third World governments must promote population control, and must be induced or pressed to do so by earmarking foreign aid for this purpose and by favouring governments pursuing such measures. Such policies already operate. They are reviewed critically in Professor Julian Simon's masterly book *The Ultimate Resource*, especially chapter 21. And also more briefly in my book *Equality, The Third World and Economic Delusion*, chapter 3.[2]

The compulsory sterilisation of hundreds of thousands of people in India in 1975-7 was perhaps the extreme case to date. On 16th April 1976 the Government of India published a statement entitled *National Population Policy* after stating that the population problem was both so formidable and so urgent that education was too slow to solve it and compulsion was required by a direct assault on it: "We are of the view that where a

State legislature . . . decides that the time is right and it is necessary to pass legislation for compulsory sterilisation, it may do so." More than six million people were sterilised in India in July to December 1976, many thousands forcibly.[3] The horrible methods and results of this programme encouraged by the West have been reliably reported in publications notably sympathetic to the Third World, such as the *New Scientist* (London) and the *Washington Post*.[4]

These ideas and policies rest on the following explicit or clearly implicit assumptions: economic performance and progress depend critically on resources per head, primarily land, but also capital; income per head is a reliable measure of economic well-being and can serve as its proxy; population trends can be reliably forecast decades ahead; Third World people do not know about birth control and procreate heedless of consequences; and the West is entitled or obliged to force them to change their reproductive habits.

These ideas go counter to simple evidence and basic moral principles.

*   *   *

Both economic history and the contemporary scene make clear that the conventional reasoning fails to identify the principal factors behind economic achievement and progress or else these factors do not interact in the manner assumed, or both.

Rapid population growth has not inhibited economic progress either in the West or in the contemporary Third World. The population of the Western World has more than quadrupled since the middle of the 18th century. Real income

---

"Rapid population growth has not inhibited economic progress either in the West or in the contemporary Third World."

---

per head is estimated to have increased by at least the factor of five. Most of the increase in incomes took place when population increased as fast, or faster than in most of the contemporary less-developed world. Similarly, in what is now called the Third World, population growth has often gone hand-in-hand with rapid material advance. In the 1890s Malaya was a sparsely-populated area of hamlets and fishing villages. By the 1930s, long before foreign aid or formal economic planning, it had become a country with large cities, extensive commerce and agricultural and mining operations. The population rose from about one and a half million to about six million; the number of Malays from about one to about two and a half million. The much larger population had much higher material standards and lived longer than the small numbers of the 1890s. Since World War Two a number of LDC's have combined rapid population increase with rapid, even spectacular economic growth for decades on end—witness Taiwan, Hong Kong, Malaysia, Kenya, the Ivory Coast, Mexico, Colombia, Brazil, among others.

Shortage of land and of investible resources is not a critical obstacle to economic achievement and progress. In particular, sustained prosperity (as distinct from occasional windfalls) owes little or nothing to natural resources—witness in the past Holland, much of it drained from the sea by the 17th century; Venice, a wealthy world power built on a few mud flats; and now West Germany, Switzerland, Japan, Singapore, Hong Kong and Taiwan, to name only the most obvious examples.

Conversely, amidst abundant land and vast natural resources, the Indians before Columbus remained wretchedly poor without domestic animals and without even the wheel when much of Europe, with far less land, was already rich.

Again, most of Africa and Latin America and much of Asia is sparsely-populated. Many millions of extremely poor people have abundant cultivable land. Shortage of land, actually or potentially cultivable, does not explain the famines in thinly-populated African countries such as Ethiopia, Uganda, Tanzania, Zaire and the Sahel, nor the extreme backwardness of the Indian populations of central and South America, or of the Pygmies and Aborigines in Asia and Africa. In many of these regions land is a free good.

Over much of the Third World extreme sparseness of the population obstructs the economic advance of enterprising people. It presents obstacles more effective than those supposedly presented by population pressure. It circumscribes the scope for enterprise by precluding the construction of transport facilities and communi-

---

". . . sustained prosperity (as distinct from occasional windfalls) owes little or nothing to natural resources. . . . Nor is shortage of capital a critical obstacle to progress. . . . Spread of knowledge, changes in attitudes and habits, redeployment of resources, technical change . . . these have been far more important as independent variables in economic advance. . . ."

---

cations and retarding the spread of markets and of new ideas and methods.

Incidentally, abundance of cultivable land is quite compatible with clamour for land reform and confiscation of established farms and plantations developed and improved by the efforts and savings of productive people. Who would not welcome a free gift of valuable assets?

Conversely, many of the most prosperous areas of the Third World are very densely-populated, even where the land is not inherently fertile. Examples include Taiwan, Hong Kong, Singapore and parts of Malaysia.

Nor is shortage of capital a critical obstacle to progress. If it were, large numbers of very poor people could not have become prosperous within a few years, as they have done the world over, as, for instance, the immigrant communities in North America and South East Asia. Even very poor people can and often do generate capital.

They can do so by sacrificing leisure for work, transferring labour and land to more productive use (e.g. from subsistence production to cash crops) and penniless traders, often illiterate, have accumulated capital by opening up local markets.

Moreover, as a factor in economic progress, the quality of investment is more significant than its volume. Expenditure does not become productive by being termed investment. Apart from much other evidence, this is plain from the numerous prestige projects in the Third World. And even when investment spending issues in productive capital formation, it is pertinent that physical capital formation is not a major factor in long-term development. Kuznets has estimated that increase in physical capital and in labour together accounted for less than one-tenth of long-term growth in the West over the last two centuries.

Spread of knowledge, changes in attitudes and habits, redeployment of resources, technical change (often confused with the accumulation of capital), these have been far more important as independent variables in economic advance than capital formation, let alone the volume of investible funds which often does not yield productive capital.

In all societies beyond the simplest subsistence stage, there are, and always have been, wide differences in economic attainment and income among individuals and groups with access to the same physical resources, notably land. Evident examples of such group differences in the same country include those between Chinese, Indians and Malays in Malaysia; Chinese and others elsewhere in South East Asia; Parsees, Jains, Marwari and others in India; Greeks and Turks in Cyprus; Asians and Africans in East and Central Africa; Ibo and others in Nigeria, and Chinese, Lebanese and West Indians in the Caribbean.

In many of these instances the most prosperous groups were discriminated against in access to land and often barred from owning it. Again, in South East Asia, the Chinese with higher incomes on average live in more densely-populated areas than the Thais, Burmese and Malays. Similarly, examples could be cited from the West, notably Huguenots, Jews and Nonconformists.

Such situations and relationships could not emerge if physical resources were critical determinants of prosperity and progress.

* * *

In current public discourse more specific adverse effects of population growth are often also alleged. These include prospective shortage of food; exhaustion of minerals; and emergence of large-scale unemployment. These apprehensions rest on invalid notions such as that methods of production and patterns of consumption do not respond to resource and availabilities; that labour and capital cannot be substituted for land in production or consumption, that there will be no technical progress; and that people procreate regardless of circumstances. I shall not discuss these issues here, partly because of lack of time and space, and also because they have been examined in detail by Professor Simon and myself in the books I referred to earlier. But I think I must state straight away that the much-publicized current famines in the Third World have nothing to do with shortage of land. They do not occur in the densely-populated areas of the Far East and elsewhere but in the sparsely-populated regions of Africa, especially Ethiopia, Uganda and the Sahel. They reflect the extreme backwardness and precarious nature of these subsistence economies, there much exacerbated by such policies and circumstances as suppression of private trade, with consequent absence of reserve stocks and trading links; persecution, even expulsion of productive groups, especially ethnic minorities; large-scale confiscation of property; forcible collectivisation; restriction on the inflow of capital and on the import of farming implements and of consumer goods; large-scale civil conflict and absence of public security. In some instances, maintenance of wasteful tribal systems of land tenure has also inhibited productive agriculture.

* * *

Per capita income, usually unstandardised for age composition, is widely used as an index of

---

"... possession of children [is] a psychic income, which is clearly a major component of human satisfaction. ..."

---

economic welfare, or even of well-being as such. Among other defects this practice ignores the psychic income derived from health, prolongation of life and possession of children, a psychic income, which is clearly a major component of human satisfaction as is evident from the readiness of people to pay for services to have their health improved, and their own lives and those of their children and parents prolonged.

This practice issues in evident anomalies. The birth of a child immediately reduces income per head within the family and also in the country as a whole. Do the parents feel worse-off? Would they be happier if they could have no children or if some of them died?

The relatively large proportion of children and of old people in some societies, especially of children in LDC's, is often decried as the burden of dependency. This terminology implies that children are merely a cost or a burden and not a source of satisfaction; and further, that survival into old age benefits no one, not even the survivors. It disregards also both the current and prospective economic contribution of children to the incomes and support of the parents.

High fertility in LDC's is often said to result in lives so miserable among the poor as not to be worth living. Similar opinions were often heard in the 19th century about the poor in Britain. This goes counter to simple observation and to widely-accepted ethics. Even the poor prefer to

---

"The relatively large proportion . . . of children in LDC's is often decried as the burden of dependency. This terminology implies that children are merely a cost or a burden and not a source of satisfaction. . . . It disregards also both the current and prospective economic contribution of children. . . . In the Third World, as in the West, the great majority of parents want the children they have."

---

live rather than not to live as is shown by their decision to remain alive.[5]

The ideas that population growth obstructs economic advance, that per capita income is a proxy for welfare, that children are only a burden, and that the lives of the very poor are not worth living, lead into the allegations that people in the Third World do not know about contraception, are at the mercy of uncontrollable sexual drives, and procreate heedless of consequences.

In fact, people in the Third World both know about birth control, and usually have access to cheap contraceptives. In most Third World societies, fertility is well below fecundity. Traditional methods of birth control were freely practised in societies much more backward than those with high fertility in contemporary LDC's.

For many decades now cheap Western style goods such as hardware, cosmetics, soft drinks, watches, cameras and many others have been conspicuous trade goods in South East Asia, South Asia, the Middle East, West Africa and Latin America. Soon after becoming available in the West the transistor radio was ubiquitous in South Asia and the Middle East, Latin America and in African cities. On the other hand, condoms, inter-uterine devices and the pill, even when heavily subsidised, have so far spread slowly in the Third World, long after their extensive use in the West (and also long after the decline in Third World mortality, which suggests that large families there are not wanted merely to replace children who have died young or may die young). Indeed, these contraceptives are often absent where sophisticated articles of feminine hygiene are on sale. All this suggests strongly that the demand for cheap Western contraceptives is limited, either because people do not want to restrict their families, or prefer other ways of doing so. In the Third World, as in the West, the great majority of parents want the children they have. Children give satisfaction; they are outlets for affection; and they enable people to project themselves into the future. They often also contribute significantly to family income, serve as support for old age and sometimes bring prestige and influence. In all these contexts, the benefits to the parents outweigh the costs; and the benefit from one highly-successful child exceeds the cost of the others.

Thus in the Third World the children who are born are generally desired. They are certainly avoidable. To deny this amounts to saying that Third World parents procreate heedless of consequences. This view treats people with unwarranted condescension or contempt, which in turn soon issues in coercion.

* * *

From Malthus to McNamara ambitious forecasts of long-term population trends have been an integral part of recurrent population scares. They are prominent in the current insistence on Third World population control. Yet for many reasons of which I can list only some, only the roughest forecasts of long-term population trends in the Third World are warranted.

Over the decades, major political, cultural and economic changes are bound to occur in much of the Third World. Both the changes and their demographic impact are unpredictable. This applies even to mortality trends, and more so to fertility trends. People do respond in their reproductive habits to changed conditions but unpredictably so, which compounds the uncertainties of the changes themselves. This applies particularly in the context of such a huge and deeply diverse aggregate as the Third World. The responses of people are often unexpected, or at least contrary to popular belief. Thus in recent decades in some LDC's economic improvement has resulted in higher fertility. Again, in some LDC's urban and rural fertilities are about the same, while in other countries there are wide differences. The relationship between fertility, social class and occupation is also much more varied in the Third World than in the West.[6]

> ". . . systematic restriction of family size in the Third World is practised primarily by women who have adopted Western attitudes towards child-bearing and child-rearing, as a result of exposure to Western education, media and contacts."

There is, however, one relationship of considerable generality which has been emphasised by Professor John C. Caldwell, and is based on his findings in Africa. This is that systematic restriction of family size in the Third World is practised primarily by women who have adopted Western attitudes towards child-bearing and child-rearing, as a result of exposure to Western education, media and contacts. Their attitude to fertility control does not depend on income, status or urbanisation, but on modernisation (which as Caldwell rightly observes is really a euphemism for Westernisation). This conclusion, which accords with common sense and observation, seems to apply widely in the Third World.[7]

Caldwell's conclusion is much more plausible and solidly-based than the widely-held view that higher incomes as such lead to reduced fertility. Higher incomes and lower fertility are often,

though by no means always, associated, particularly in the West and in the westernised parts of the Third World. But it is not the case that higher incomes as such lead to smaller families. Both the higher incomes and the smaller families reflect greater ambition for material welfare for oneself and one's family. If parental incomes are increased as a result of subsidies or windfalls, without a change in attitudes, the parents are likely to have more children, not fewer.

Deficiencies in vital statistics also preclude reliable forecasts. In much of the Third World there is no registration of births and deaths, and even where there is, it is often seriously incomplete. In many countries estimates of the size of the population vary greatly. The population of Nigeria was officially estimated in 1963 at 55.6 million; Professor Peter Kilby put it at 37.1 million. At present (November 1984) estimates of the population of Ethiopia range from 32.6 million to 44 million. Estimates of the population of the People's Republic of China differ by many millions. These considerations should help to place into perspective such practices as forecasts of the population of the world for the year 2000 to the nearest million, or the publication of statistics of the growth of income or of agricultural production per head in LDC's to fractions of one per cent.

Some unambitious and broad conclusions about Third World population trends over the next few decades may be made. Although the speed and extent of Westernisation are uncertain, the process is likely to make some headway. This would result in some decline in age-specific fertility. But the large proportion of young people and the prevailing reproduction rates will ensure significant increases in population in the principal regions of the Third World over the next few decades. Population growth of the less developed world as a whole is unlikely to fall much be-

> "The economic achievement and general well-being of the peoples of the Third World will not be a matter of their number, but of personal, cultural and political factors."

low two per cent and may for some years continue around two and a half per cent.

More specific forecasts would be conjectural. Nor are they necessary. The economic achievement and general well-being of the peoples of the Third World will not be a matter of their number, but of personal, cultural and political factors. It will not depend on numbers, but on conduct, including that of Governments.[8]

*   *   *

There is no case, either on moral or on economic grounds, to induce or press Third World Governments officially to promote population control.

Some advocates of this policy, but by no means all, and certainly not the most influential, maintain that they intend only to widen the opportunities of people by assisting in the spread of contraceptive knowledge.

As I have noted, Third World people know about birth control and have access to cheap contraceptives. Further dissemination of informa-

> "... subsidised distribution of contraceptives may do little harm, though the financial cost may not be negligible. But it may well induce insecurity and tension if accompanied by insistent official propaganda against prevailing mores. . . . More important, in many LDC's, especially in Asia and Africa . . . advice, education and persuasion in practice shade into coercion."

tion, or even subsidised distribution of contraceptives may do little harm, though the financial cost may not be negligible. But it may well induce insecurity and tension if accompanied by insistent official propaganda against prevailing mores. This, incidentally, is what happened in Iran.

More important, in many LDCs, especially in Asia and Africa, is that advice, education and persuasion in practice shade into coercion. In

> "We should hesitate before putting pressure on people to radically and rapidly alter their conduct in their most private and vital concerns. . . .
>
> "An altogether different course is open to those who wish for wider voluntary adoption of family limitation. This is extension of the range of external commercial contacts available to ordinary people in the Third World, especially contacts with the West."

most of these societies people are, by tradition, more subject to authority than in the West. And especially in recent years the prospects of many people have come to depend on official favours. Promotion in the Civil Service, allocation of licences (including even to operate taxis in parts of India), access to subsidised credit, official housing and other facilities have all been linked at times to restriction of family size. Forcible mass sterilisation in India was only the limiting case.

Such policies must provoke acute anxiety, tension and conflict, and raise most serious moral and political problems. If pressed home, they leave behind a dejected, inert population.

An altogether different course is open to those who wish for wider voluntary adoption of family limitation. This is extension of the range of external commercial contacts available to ordinary people in the Third World, especially contacts with the West. Such contacts have been powerful agents of voluntary, uncoerced changes in attitudes and mores, especially those harmful to economic advance. Similar results can also confidently be expected in this area, brought about gradually, and without coercion. We should hesitate before putting pressure on people to radically and rapidly alter their conduct in their most private and vital concerns.

Notes

1. Robert S. McNamara, *One Hundred Countries, Two Billion People: The Dimensions of Development*, London, Pall Mall Press, 1973, pp. 31, 45-6

2. Princeton University Press, 1981; Princeton, N.J. London, Weidenfeld and Nicolson, 1981, and Methuen and Co., 1983 (paperback); Cambridge, Mass. Harvard University Press, 1982.

3. Paul Demeny, 'Bucharest, Mexico City and Beyond'; *Population Notes 55*, The Population Council, New York, September 1984. This is a highly informative and perceptive article which reviews some of the most widely-canvassed ideas and adopted policies in this field.

4. e.g. J. Hanlan and A. Agrawal, 'Mass Sterilization at Gunpoint', *New Scientist*, London, 5 May 1977. They write: "The Western Aid Agencies . . . either kept quiet or applauded the sterilization programme. World Bank President, Robert McNamara, took time off from his busy schedule during his Indian visit to call upon the Indian Health and Family Planning Minister to congratulate him for the Indian Government's political will and determination in popularising family planning. This was during November 1976 at the height of the compulsory sterilization campaign." See also *Washington Post*, 4 July 1977 for an account of forcible mass sterilization in India.

5. 'The weariest and most loathed wordly life
   That age, ache, penury and imprisonment
   Can lay on nature, is a paradise
   To what we fear of death'
   (*Measure for Measure*, III, I)

6. Findings on these and related matters by Professors W. Peterson, John Caldwell, and Dr. J. Kocher, are summarized in *Equality, The Third World and Economic Delusion*, loc cit.

7. Caldwell's conclusion is linked to his theory of the reversal of the intergenerational flow of resources which occurs when the primitive or traditional society gives way to the transitional society; cf. John C. Caldwell 'Towards a Restatement of Demographic Transition Theory', *Population and Development Review*, September-December 1976.

8. At this point it seems necessary to forestall a somewhat technical but often-heard objection or reservation. This is that people in the Third World have larger families than is socially desirable because the parents do not themselves bear the full cost of raising the children. There are adverse financial externalities from large families, so that taxpayers subsidise parents.

Such effects are more significant in the West than in the Third World because the relevant public expenditures are less in the latter. For instance, schools can be and often are simple inexpensive structures. However, in so far as the children will support the old, state spending for that purpose is correspondingly less. Again, these externalities do not depend simply on family size. For instance, a small family may be subsidised if the children receive publicly-funded University education, while a much larger family may not be subsidised if the parents pay for the cost of schooling. In any case, if financial externalities are deemed objectionable, they can be remedied by reducing the expenditure, or modifying its incidence. They do not call for forcible reduction in family size.

Western observers who urge Third World population control also often urge more aid to the poor, including those with large families. But if parenthood is subsidised, people are less likely to restrict family size than they would otherwise. This is so because the higher incomes do not result from a change in motivation.

Addendum

I have confined this essay to matters arising directly out of the so-called Third World population explosion. But I do not want to leave the subject of world population trends without noting another, related, issue.

In recent years, reproduction rates in the West have declined considerably, especially so in Western Europe. Within the so-called Third World, fertility rates differ substantially, but fertility and reproduction rates are generally much higher than in the West. If these differences persist, then the population of the West (including Japan and Australasia) will over the years shrink considerably compared with Asia, Africa and Latin America, which eventually must have wide political and cultural results.

I can neither develop nor even conjecture about these horizons here, but they should not be left unmentioned in a discussion on contemporary population trends and policies.

Commentaries

ALLEN KELLEY
*James B. Duke Professor of Economics, Associate
Director, Center for Demographic Studies,
Duke University.*

MR. KELLEY: There are a lot of very interesting people around the table, and I myself would like to hear from some of them, so I'll keep my comments brief.

I think that the papers that have been presented are extremely rich and provide a lot of insights that are important in the population area. I

"One of the interesting aspects of these papers is I think they are pointing the direction for a revisionist interpretation of the role of population in economic development. It is quite clear that the population debate is entering a new phase, and this is all to the good. The population debate was settled in the 1970s. Population was unequivocally bad for the process of economic development; there were virtually no redeeming qualities in it. This has changed in the 1980s. . . ."

---

would like to offer two or three general comments that will, I hope, assist in putting them in context. One of the interesting aspects of these papers is I think they are pointing the direction for a revisionist interpretation of the role of population in economic development. It is quite clear that the population debate is entering a new phase, and this is all to the good.

The population debate was settled in the 1970s. Population was unequivocally bad for the process of economic development; there were virtually no redeeming qualities in it. This has changed in the 1980s, and one asks the question, Why? One of the reasons is that birth rates are coming down in many countries, but I think that there are other reasons, as well.

Two other reasons, I think, should be cited. One is that in the last two decades, we have learned a lot more from research about the role of population in development. One of the more conspicuous contributors to this body of research, Julian Simon, is at the table this morning, and I think the attention he has been able to bring to the subject through the wide array of his research has been very important in this area.

But there is another reason, and I think Timothy King, who is a senior population analyst at the World Bank, put his finger on it. There has been a tendency—and I quote him—"of many of those most concerned with population to exaggerate its significance." And this is, remember, a senior population analyst, with an excellent command of the literature, at the World Bank, an organization which over the recent years has been rather anti-natal.

A final development that has changed the debate is that many of the previous arguments that were used in the anti-natal position have not been sustained by empirical evidence. This has, I think, been clearly revealed in the last two decades.

". . . many of the previous arguments that were used in the anti-natal position have not been sustained by empirical evidence."

So in brief, I feel a revisionist interpretation is beginning to emerge, which places population in its proper perspective. Population is neither a villain nor a hero in the economic development story. It is instead an important actor in a complex plot.

Consider just two areas of the anti-natalist argument over the last two decades, and how research has clarified some of the issues involved. The famous Coale-Hoover thesis, espoused some 25 years ago and applied originally to the country of India, said basically that rapid population growth leads to a relatively large proportion of children in the population, and that this diverts household income away from saving and toward consumption. Now, on its face value, this is a very plausible hypothesis. The issue is whether, number one, it is quantitatively important, and number two, even if it were quantitatively important, is physical capital formation a primary ingredient in explaining the process of economic development? Both Professors Preston and Bauer have cast severe question this morning with respect to the latter proposition. And with respect to the previous proposition, I would simply note that two other writers—and I am going to quote them here—have cast doubt on the proposition that large numbers of children do indeed curtail the availability of savings resources in Third World countries.

Timothy King at the World Bank has said, "In the litany of anti-natalist argument, this one bears little weight. It is unlikely that the proportion of children in the population is very important at all."

And Geoff McNicoll of the Population Council in a recent review asked the question, "What can be said about net savings and investment impacts of rapid population growth? The answer is 'Very little'."

In other words, the foundation of the early anti-natalist arguments against population—that is, the arguments suggesting that population growth will deter the rate of economic savings, capital formation and growth—has just plain not been sustained in 20 or 25 years of empirical research, both at the micro-economic level and at the macro-economic level.

A second argument, I think, bears mentioning, and this is only two of half a dozen I'd like to talk about, but I am only going to mention two, just for illustrative purposes. This one relates to food production, which has been a subject of international interest of recent days, with the dire situation in Ethiopia and incipient problems in other African countries, as well.

Basically, the anti-natalists have argued that diminishing returns to land and natural resources turn out to be quantitatively important, and one way of resolving this food balance problem would be to reduce the demands on land through the demands for food.

The World Bank, in its most recent report, one that was participated in very actively by Nancy Birdsall, notes the following facts: Number one, the world will be able, with current technologies and expanding technologies, to feed itself well into the 21st century, given population projections as we know them presently.

Secondly, most of the Third World countries will be able to be self-sufficient in the year 2000 in the area of food, although several of the Sub-Saharan African countries will not, and will require external assistance.

Thirdly, the possibilities for expanding food production are in fact quite substantial.

And finally, the greatest constraints on agricultural production relate not to population, but

---

". . . the greatest constraints on agricultural production relate not to population, but rather to the need to expand production, and these constraints are in the areas of government policy."

---

rather, to the need to expand production, and these constraints are in the areas of government policy.

Now, I think we should not be complacent about food shortages. These are dire problems, and one must face them seriously and with resolve. Food crises will continue, and in fact, I fear they are going to worsen. But I think a couple of points need to be made.

Lord Peter Bauer mentioned one of these, and that is that food famines themselves have not usually been the result of lack of production, but rather a function of entitlements to existing production—the availability of income, the claims on food made available by governments, and other social mechanisms.

A second point I want to make is that the greatest constraint on expansion of food availability in Third World countries is the lack of incentives to expand production. Governments typically twist the terms of trade against the farmer. They tax the farming input, they tax the farming outputs. It is surprising that the farm sector does as well as it does in many Third World countries, given the incentive structures that farmers face.

The World Bank in its World Economic Development Report last year noted that price distortions—and I'm referring here not just to food prices, but to other price distortions, as well—explain approximately one-third of the variation in output performance in many Third World countries.

Now, if we are truly interested in the problem of food balance, we should not be overly concerned with just one side of the story, that is,

---

"... if we are truly interested in the problem of food balance, we should not be overly concerned with just one side of the story, that is, worrying about demand. We should worry about supply as well."

---

worrying about demand. We should worry about supply as well. And one of the interesting facts here is that constraining demand by constraining population, while valid, will take years and years and maybe decades. Whereas removing some price distortions, overvalued exchange rates, terms of trade distortions between the agricultural sector and the urban sectors, could in fact be implemented virtually within weeks or months, and some of these problems could be rapidly on

their way to resolution, although we all recognize that the political realities of doing this will not be easy.

Let me conclude with a couple of observations as to where I perceive this population debate going, and about what I view as a rather upbeat situation. Look, for instance, at the changes in population perspective at the World Bank over the last decade. Lord Bauer's paper included a beautiful quote reflecting the position of the Bank eleven years ago with respect to population. It is a quote by Robert McNamara in which he likened population growth to the hazards of a thermo-nuclear war, in which he stated, "The greatest single obstacle to the economic and social advancement of the majority of the peoples of the underdeveloped world is rapid population growth . . . The threat of unmanageable population pressures is much like that of nuclear war . . . both threats can and will have catastrophic consequences."

Just a decade later, last year, the new President of the World Bank, referring to the Third World countries, and the poorest of the Third World countries in particular, made the following statement: "The poverty of these areas cannot be blamed on rapid population growth alone. The causes of poverty go well beyond population change. Nor will reducing population growth alone ensure their rapid transformation."

In short, I think we should take seriously what we have learned, or what I hope we have learned, about what the determinants of economic progress are in the Third World, and place population in a balanced perspective whereby the causes and not the symptoms of the problems are treated.

JULIAN SIMON
University of Maryland; Adjunct Scholar, Heritage Foundation; author of The Economics of Population Growth *and* The Ultimate Resource.

MR. SIMON: Before starting, I'd like to second everything that Allen Kelley just said, most especially with respect to government interference in food supply.

I'll address myself to earlier statements by the speakers, because the texts of their talks weren't available. By now, Peter Bauer's views on

Mr. Simon

the economic development of poorer countries have been widely accepted among economists, replacing the earlier planning models that had been popular in the 1950s and the 1960s. An important reason for the ascendance of his views is that events in a wide variety of countries that tried the earlier planning models have turned out disastrously.

Because I so heartily agree with his views, and because you just heard them for yourselves, I will say no more.

It is, however, worth noting a major change in Lord Bauer's views over the course of his books. If I read him correctly, he has shifted from the belief that population growth is bad, to the view that it is neutral or beneficial in the long run. And many others have been changing their minds on this subject, also. In 1974, the then Governor of California said: "Unless major efforts are made to reduce population growth, vast numbers of people will face severe famine and misery." And in the second Reagan-Mondale debate, you heard the same Mr. Reagan state quite the opposite.

Now, perhaps this intellectual evolution occurred because the resource shortages that had been forecast for the 1970s and 1980s by those who called for population control have not occurred. Instead, we have a glut of most raw materials. As you have heard, even the World Bank has abandoned resource scarcity and shifted to the supply of education as the supposed key evil consequence of population growth—about which more, later.

Rafael Salas and his U.N. Fund for Popula-

tion Activities advocate central world planning of fertility and population growth. Despite his very careful language, this proposition is unmistakeable, at least to me. Consider, for example, the official press release to the World Population Conference. Quote: "Salas called for the continuation and strengthening of global population programs. These programs, he said, should be sustained, in his own words, 'until the promise of stabilization is within sight.' He asked the delegates to"—again, his words in the press release—"'agree on global strategies that can complement national population policies. Only the determined, rational and humane national population policies of countries can bring about a more satisfying future for the forthcoming generations'."

And in his report on the World Population Plan of Action, Mr. Salas writes, quote: "Population change is considered a legitimate subject of direct governmental intervention. And all countries will continue to integrate their population measures and programs into their social and economic goals. Governments will take the measures they deem necessary concerning fertility levels." And he refers to "motivational actions" and "population education" as appropriate tools.

These statements make clear that the UNFPA is calling for a program much different than simply helping individual couples attain the number of children they wish by ensuring a supply of contraceptive information and devices. They are saying that population must be stabilized whether or not that would be the outcome of individual couples making private decisions, even though Mr. Salas frequently repeats that the programs must, in his words, "guarantee the dignity and freedom of all humans."

An ambiguous phrase apparently resolves the apparent contradiction. He talks about "giving all people the knowledge and the means to bring forth only the children for whom they can provide the fullest opportunities for growth." That could mean, for example, that unless a family has enough income to provide for the children what the government decides are "the fullest opportunities for growth," there would be grounds to prevent the family from having the child.

Now, if the UNFPA considers this an unfair inference about their program, they have only to foreswear calling for a reduction in population growth rates and, instead, call for "giving people the knowledge and the means"—period. And they would make themselves clearer if they would condemn the coercive programs in China.

At the bottom of the UNFPA's outlook, just as with the World Bank and USAID and our State Department, is the assumption that, in Mr. Salas' words, "Rapid population growth has made it extremely difficult for governments to achieve their development goals. Population stabilization will make it less difficult for the developing countries to improve their levels of living."

No notice is taken by the UNFPA or, for a recent example, the recent World Bank Report, that there is a large body of scientific studies, to which you have several times heard reference this morning, showing an absence of the supposed negative relationship between population

---

". . . there is a large body of scientific studies, to which you have several times heard reference this morning, showing an absence of the supposed negative relationship between population growth and economic growth in the long run. And the effect of higher population density actually seems to be positive."

---

growth and economic growth in the long run. And the effect of higher population density actually seems to be positive. Even the supposed diminution of education per student in the presence of faster population growth is either small or nonexistent, according to the scientific literature.

And all of the evidence for hundreds and even thousands of years shows natural resources to be getting more available—that is, less costly—even as population has multiplied and resource use has multiplied even faster.

So I ask, therefore, how can Mr. Salas, Mr. Clausen of the World Bank, Mr. McPherson of AID, and other policymakers continue to take no notice of this body of scientific literature.

Perhaps it is that, as people used to say of Freudian psychoanalysis, they feel that the human problem is too serious for it to be deterred by conventional scientific evidence.

Turning now to Sam Preston, let me first applaud his remarks about family planning programs.

Now, I believe the central benefit of more people in a more developed world is that there are more ingenious people to invent new ideas. I believe there is much empirical evidence for this. But Mr. Preston finds this to be a logical fallacy. He compares two situations with the same total

---

". . . the central benefit of more people in a more developed world is that there are more ingenious people to invent new ideas. I believe there is much empirical evidence for this."

---

number of persons—one case in which the persons live simultaneously, against another in which the same total number of persons are spaced out over a long period of time. He figures there is no difference in human welfare between these two situations, because the same living-standard improving inventions will arise in each case, and at the same point in the life of each society.

One drawback to this comparison is that it takes no account of the economist's standard assumption that events that will happen in the near future have a higher present value than the same events in the farther future because of discounting and time preference. But much more important, the relevant comparison is not between situations with the same total number of persons over time, but rather between cases with more and less people at any given time.

The only assumption that could make sense of Sam's model is that the supply of sustenance is absolutely fixed, and the moment our supply is used up, the race dies out. Such an assumption is so contrary to everything we know, that it would seem to render his objection without merit.

If this is the strongest objection to the argument that more people yield more innovations and higher living standards, which Mr. Preston attributes to Simon Kuznets and to me, which I would attribute to William Petty several hundred years ago, then it would seem that this argument is secure.

In closing, I would like to offer this observation. We certainly need to struggle at solving the problems that confront us. But we should also welcome the scarcity problems that are caused by increasing population and rising incomes, because if problems do not arise, solutions will not be evoked. And the entire process of scarcity problems arising and then getting solved almost always leaves us better off than if the problems had never arisen. If population had not increased about 8,000 years ago and made hunting and gathering become less productive, we would be having wild roots, rabbits, and berries for lunch instead of supping in the manner to which we have become accustomed.

*NANCY BIRDSALL
Population, Health and Nutrition Branch, The World Bank; led production of 1984 World Development Report *on population.*

MS. BIRDSALL: I will comment primarily on Lord Bauer's paper, which I find interesting and provocative, as so much of Lord Bauer's work is, but highly flawed. And I disagree with the conclusion. Let me begin by pointing out three areas where I agree with Lord Bauer's observation, but disagree with his implied conclusion. Then I'll go on to summarize some themes from the World Bank's *World Development Report.*

"The real issue is not whether population is the principal problem but whether it is one among several development problems which needs to be addressed."

My first area of agreement with Lord Bauer is that rapid population growth is not the principal problem of underdevelopment. But to say rapid population growth is not the prime obstacle to development is not to say it is no problem at all. In fact, despite the sometimes exaggerated rhetoric about population as a problem, the amount of money actually spent on population programs is tiny. The real issue is not whether population is the principal problem but whether it is one among several development problems which needs to be addressed.

The second point on which I can agree easily

is that there is no fundamental problem of scarcity of natural resources at the global level. There is no imminent disaster because of some limitations of what people call the carrying capacity of mother earth. Indeed, the population problem is not a problem of too many people or of density or crowding, as the examples of Hong Kong, the Netherlands, and Japan demonstrate. The neo-Malthusian argument about natural resources, and crowding, is a straw man.

But contrary to Lord Bauer's assertion, the *rate* of growth in developing countries is faster than *ever* experienced in the past by the industrial countries. Except for a brief period in America, the population growth rate exceeded 1.5 percent for only a decade or so in England. The higher growth rate in America—of about 2 percent—was due to immigration, which does not impose the burden that high birth rates and a youthful population impose.

The third point on which I agree is Lord Bauer's observation that poor people have good reasons for wanting many children. I'll return to this point in a moment and explain why I disagree with his implicit conclusion.

Now let me try and describe very briefly the major themes of the World Development Report. The rapid pace of population growth puts tremendous pressure on limited investment resources in poor countries. It makes it more difficult for countries to manage their limited investment resources.

Consider the example of education. Rapid population growth as a result of high fertility means that in developing countries 40-50 percent of populations are typically under the age of 15. That means there are relatively fewer working-age people to support the younger people. It is thus more difficult to maintain investment in education. Many countries have made tremendous efforts in the last 20-30 years to increase their rates of enrollment, and, as Sam Preston and Julian Simon have pointed out, there is not a negative association between enrollment rates in the developing world and the rate of population growth. We do not know, unfortunately, what might have been with somewhat less pressure to expand schooling systems so rapidly.

A second example is the agricultural sector. In most countries of tropical Africa and much of South Asia, 70 percent of the labor force is still working in agriculture. Because those countries

---

*A last minute difficulty prevented Ms. Birdsall from arriving at the conference. The remarks she would have delivered have here been inserted into the conference record.

have rapid population growth, even with considerable migration to cities, the number of people who will be depending on the land for their livelihood is likely to at least double in the next 40 years. Investments in agriculture will have to double at least and hopefully more than double if productivity per worker and thus income are going to increase. This is particularly important in countries where the land frontier is limited—where more and more people will depend on the existing land. Unfortunately, just getting the prices right and improving farmer incentives is not likely to be enough. Investment in fertilizer, in new irrigation systems, in technology, will also be necessary—all at the same time investment in education also needs to be increasing. Changes in land tenure systems, adoption of conservation measures, adaptation to local soil conditions of scientific advances, require concerted and organized social effort. They will not be initiated spontaneously by individual farmers. All this is possible, but more difficult to do when there is constant stress on the political and economic system because of rapid population increases.

The second theme of the Report is that there are appropriate public policies to reduce fertility in developing countries. By appropriate I mean fair, noncoercive, complementary to other development programs, and eminently affordable. In the Report we asked the questions: Why should there be public intervention in any area of human life that is clearly such a private one, where very fundamental human values are at stake? We suggest two reasons. First is what you might call a gap between the private gains from high fertility and the social gains—what Preston referred to as an externality. As Lord Bauer correctly pointed out, the private gains from high fertility, particularly for poor people, can be substantial. For poor people, children provide sometimes the only safe means of old age security. Wherever infant mortality is high it makes sense to have extra children to guard against the possibility that one or two may die. Children can work and add to family income. Where educational opportunities are limited, parents do not face the immediate cost of sending their children to school. In parts of Asia where women are excluded from the labor force, a son may be critical for old-age security; the plight of widows in parts of South Asia can be a very pitiful one.

Yet many poor couples in developing countries, even as they want to have many children themselves, wish that their neighbors would have fewer so that their own children would face less competition in the future for school places, land and jobs. This attitude in itself implies a gap between private and social gains.

So I agree with Lord Bauer that it may make sense for poor people to have many children. But I disagree that government should do nothing. Government provides a mechanism by which people can get together and make a kind of social contract with each other: we will, through the mechanism of government, institute policies that change our environment in ways that encourage lower fertility, inducing us and all of our neighbors to have fewer children. I am not talking here about coercion, but about changing the environment so people themselves choose fewer children. Better health care to reduce infant mortality and more education for women are two of the most obvious changes.

There is a second reason that public policy is justified. And that is that many people in developing countries are having more children than they want. Lord Bauer seems to suggest that people are able to do whatever they want in this respect *at no cost*. Yet in parts of the developing world, couples who want to limit their fertility face grim alternatives: abortion, unsafe means of contraception, infanticide. For many couples it makes sense to have the extra child rather than undergo such a cost. Information about modern family planning does not spread easily; even in this country, new contraceptives of the last few years are little known, because of cultural mores. There is in effect a market failure—partly because people don't discuss sexual matters and contraception as readily as new agricultural techniques or changes in the interest rate, partly because there is no way a private entrepreneur can capture all the benefits of spreading information about contraception, partly because of distortions in other markets—for example because modern health care itself is largely a public sector function in developing countries, and many modern contraceptives are tied to modern health care. We estimate that there are at least 65 million couples in developing countries who want no more children—but are using no form of contraception.

The third major message of the Report is that we know from the successful experience of many countries that policies and programs to reduce fertility work. They have worked rapidly in a wide range of countries at low cost. In a host of countries, fertility has come down by 30 percent, even more, in less than twenty years. That's the case not only in the rapidly-growing industrializing economies of Korea, Taiwan, Hong Kong, and Singapore, but in many countries that are still largely rural and still of low income. Fertility has fallen fast and far in Sri Lanka, Thailand, Colombia, Chile, Cuba, Costa Rica, parts of India, Mexico, and Indonesia. In Mexico and Indonesia, contraceptive use quadrupled in less than a decade

---

"It is not income growth or urbanization or westernization or even a market-oriented economic system which holds the key to decline in fertility. It is a powerful combination of educating women, improving health services and providing the option of safe and effective means of family planning."

---

from 10 to more than 40 percent, and is still rising. The increase started in about 1973, the year those governments began supporting services. Moreover, family planning programs have not cost much. Most governments are spending 1-2 percent at most of their public budget on family planning services.

It is not income growth or urbanization or westernization or even a market-oriented economic system which holds the key to decline in fertility. It is a powerful combination of educating women, improving health services and providing the option of safe and effective means of family planning.

Let me conclude with a word about China. I have suggested the goal of a population policy is to reconcile individual and social objectives—by altering the environment in noncoercive ways. There are two problems with what is happening in China: (1) It is not clear that there will be any obvious social gain in reducing the rate of population growth from, say, an already low 1.2 percent to 0.5 percent or less. (2) Even were there some social gain, would it be sufficient to offset the terrible private costs of the drive for a single-child family implied by the evidence of female infanticide, forced abortions and so forth? China is a re-

minder that insufficient resources for voluntary steps today may induce more governments to feel coercion, or active persuasion or whatever it might be called, is necessary in the future.

JAMES SCHALL, S.J.
Professor of Government, Georgetown University; author of Human Dignity and Human Numbers *and* Welcome Number 4,000,000,000.

FATHER SCHALL: I was struck by the first line of Professor Preston's essay stating that "Any social unit within which reproduction occurs is faced with a population problem." Since I belong to an organization in which reproduction does not legally occur, I wish to point out that voluntary organizations, too, can have various kinds of population problems, both with increase and decrease of numbers.

What I would like to do first of all is compliment this organization for this particular panel. One of my observations about universities today is that this kind of cross-fertilization of disciplines and acute critical attention to what a discipline stands for doesn't very often happen within them. You have a sociology department, and a political science department, and a theology department, and this kind of department and that kind of department, and they never really talk to each other on a fundamental level about their disciplines and issues.

Now, on this question of this conference, I would like to ask, "What is the philosophical understanding of population?"

It has been my experience that the location of contemporary discussions about the nature of tyranny and the nature of tyrannical governments is much more likely to be found in population discussions than it is in the various other parts of political and sociological theory. For example, somebody mentioned earlier today the reduction of birth rate in China without ever bringing up the question of how it was done, on what principles, and in what political context. That particular kind of attitude, it seems to me, presupposes important questions about the nature of the human being and the human enterprise over time on this earth.

I think the Holy See, in its intervention in the Mexico Conference recently, pointed out that the first question we have to ask about population is a theological and philosophical one: "What are the dignity and nature of the human person in the first place?" What we call populations are individual human beings, the plurality of human beings. Some people estimate maybe 90 to 100 billion people have existed so far on the face of this earth. What is their relationship to themselves, to each other, to the earth itself? Generally speaking, there is in both the Greek tradition and the Hebrew tradition a notion that the existence of man is the end and purpose of this earth, and therefore a legitimacy to man using this earth for his own good.

It strikes me furthermore that man ought not to be looked upon— and this is where I find one of the dangers, one of my feelings about the totalitarian aspect of certain elements in the population discussion—simply as a corporate group, a kind of abstraction of all mankind over history. Such thinking cannot capture the meaning and

---

"It strikes me . . . that man ought not to be looked upon . . . simply as a corporate group, a kind of abstraction of all mankind over history. Such thinking cannot capture the meaning and dignity in each individual human being. . . ."

---

dignity in each individual human being who lives on this earth, and who in some sense transcends the earth as such.

The philosophical implications of population discussion ought to be faced much more frankly. Namely, what is the worth of each human being?

This conference is refreshing because I think it clearly indicates movement away from the feeling that population is a kind of overriding mechanism, an overriding force which cannot be controlled, and because it is such a threatening force, all other political and social values must be subordinated to it.

In fact, it strikes me, the proper order of things is quite the other way around. We ought to go back to our philosophical and theoretical positions about man's being and reality when we

think about this, and be quite clear about what we are doing when we talk of "human numbers."

I think some of you probably noticed the

"This conference is refreshing because I think it clearly indicates movement away from the feeling that population is a kind of overriding mechanism, an overriding force which cannot be controlled, and because it is such a threatening force, all other political and social values must be subordinated to it."

---

series of essays in *The New Yorker* recently by a man by the name of Daniel Kevles, discussing the tradition of eugenics. He called it "the secular faith." In one of my classes we have been reading Plato, and Book V of Plato is the classic discussion of a certain extreme to which this theory could go. Plato told us to think about population and eugenics in their relation to the polity. But the notion that there ought to be a civil authority in charge of the quality and quantity of human beings, and that the principles at stake ought to be determined by some kind of, in the modern sense, world authority, strikes me as an extremely, extremely dangerous premise. And it is refreshing to me to hear a number of people in today's conference recognize the radical problems with such an assumption. Rather we ought to work from the premise that when mankind was given this earth, he was given it as a risk; that the

---

"The notion that there ought to be a civil authority in charge of the quality and quantity of human beings . . . strikes me as an extremely, extremely dangerous premise."

---

risk is something which mankind, without compromising his dignity at all, can bear, for his own good and that of his descendants; and that this process is a good thing, that life itself, the newness of life itself, is in fact a good thing.

Discussion

MR. WATTENBERG: Thank you, Father Schall. I'd like to open discussion now amongst our panelists. Mr. Merrick?

MR. MERRICK: My comment is directed at a point in Julian Simon's book, *The Ultimate Resource.*

One of the main themes of that book is that human ingenuity produces responses when there is stress in the balance between population and resources.

My comment is that one of the most striking recent manifestations of how that ingenuity has

---

". . . one of the most striking recent manifestations of how [human] ingenuity has operated are the efforts that have been mobilized to bring about the reduction in total fertility in developing countries from six children per woman to four, in less than a decade."

Tom Merrick

---

operated are the efforts that have been mobilized to bring about the reduction in total fertility in developing countries from six children per woman to four, in less than a decade. That mobilization of effort—which includes a great deal of scientific research on both the social and economic determinants of human fertility, as well as reproductive physiology and service delivery systems,

and the organization of both private and public initiative to increase reproductive choice—while it hasn't been without some mistakes and wrong turns, as has been pointed out in the course of the discussion, has generated a truly impressive engine of social change. As Mr. Salas has noted, this experience has provided lessons that are now being applied, for example, in extending low cost health care to mothers and children in the developing world.

To me, it is curious that one of the most striking manifestations of the Simon thesis is not recognized by its author, and I wondered if you would be willing to comment on that at some point in the discussion?

MR. WATTENBERG: We will come back to you, Julian. Werner?

MR. FORNOS: Let me first say that there is no such revolution taking place as Mr. Simon seems to point out, that an awful lot of people are turning their backs on the population problem. I don't intend to be an apologist for the population movement here today, but a world growing by 83 million people a year portends a grave threat to the world's stability, and will continue to enjoy a number one priority by people throughout the world who are deeply concerned about the quality of life and its associated deterioration as a result of lack of resources and a diminishing environment.

Now, Mr. Bauer, I don't know how you could

possibly have not come in contact with Sir Maurice Kendall, that great British statistician who went around the world with probably the largest social science research project that has ever been undertaken, the World Fertility Survey, conducted by the International Statistical Institute.

"... a world growing by 83 million people a year portends a grave threat to the world's stability, and will continue to enjoy a number one priority by people throughout the world who are deeply concerned about the quality of life and its associated deterioration as a result of lack of resources and a diminishing environment."

Werner Fornos

He pointed out that there are some 400 million women in the world who lack access to the education and the means of fertility control, in contrast to your simple statement that everybody in the Third World knows of a cheap method of family planning and how to get it. I just don't understand that. May I suggest that what we are facing is a crisis in global responsibility. We talk about development being an answer to the poverty that millions of people in the world find themselves in, yet I do not see any individuals advocating a massive increase in humanitarian assistance, willing to go to the Congress of the United States and the other industrialized democracies and tell them that they should accelerate the transfer of technology, that they should accelerate the means by which people can produce the agricultural capacity that you speak of.

I think we need to work together to address the population problem with the development problem. To go back and continually harp upon Indian sterilization abuses in 1977—I should point out that when the Janata Party came into power, it offered 5,000 rupees to anybody who came forth and could prove that they were forcibly sterilized. And even after two years in office, the opposition party was not able to bring forth one single witness that could attest and claim that 5,000 rupees.

I have just finished a 5,000-mile trip through China with independent interpretation, with a completely set itinerary of my own. I have not witnessed forced abortions or forced sterilizations, though I am sure in a nation of one billion, there probably were some abuses somewhere, just as there are abuses in our political system, and when a Senator or a secretary of the cabinet gets indicted for wrongdoing, we don't jump forth and say let's do away with democracy—

MR. WATTENBERG: Werner, are you saying that Chinese fertility policy is not coercive, the official government policy?

MR. FORNOS: The official policy that is in effect in 1984, and as I have seen it through the villages where I have visited, has very strong posters all over the place that prohibit force or coercion. There may in the past, as has been documented by NOVA, have been zealous cadres.

MR. WATTENBERG: But when a government has complete control of the education system, and the economic system, and the land system and housing and jobs and everything, and then wields carrots and sticks against the uncooperative in a totalitarian setting, isn't that coercive, *de facto*?

MR. FORNOS: It is a matter, Ben, of what is incen-

tive and disincentive practice, in an economic system that has a billion people, whose development process is deteriorating and needs to be brought to a point where the people who are alive today can enjoy just a measure of decent life.

The family planning program that has been undertaken, village after village has strong requirements for voluntarism. Yes, it does have institutional incentives, just as we have institutional incentives to get things done. We are using the economic stick and carrot on all sectors. Why can't it be used in educating people to have a smaller size family, so that the people who are born have a chance to make it in this world?

MR. EBERSTADT: Just a single comment, which won't address all of this. Mr. Fornos's remarks remind me very much of what Molotov said when he went into a pact with Nazi Germany. He said, "Fascism is a matter of taste."

MR. WATTENBERG: Next comment—Sam?

MR. BAUM: In listening to the various panelists and some of the commentators, I guess the pendulum has started to swing the other way. But as in most things, life is not just pure black and white. As Sam Preston pointed out, population growth may be a minor factor in economic development, but it is a factor. And, as he pointed out, it may be a cost-effective factor, one that we can do something about.

I also have come back from China—in fact, I met Werner Fornos at a couple of places there on our itineraries. And I guess when a society and its units have a population plan and a birth plan which allow couples to have children only when that society says they can have children, that is, I wouldn't say necessarily coercive, but it is getting toward that kind of a system. And I guess I would have to disagree a little bit with Werner on the extent of coercion in the Chinese system.

MR. WATTENBERG: Karl Zinsmeister?

MR. ZINSMEISTER: Yes, I would like to pick up on what I think is a very interesting point by Mr. Merrick. Specifically, that to some extent the response of the family planning community in the last ten years has been exactly what Julian Simon predicts. Namely, that crises produce creative thinking, and thus responses. I think it is a point

which deserves to be made that a vast majority of the international family planning effort has been honorable and decent and has simply produced information and services for people who choose to use them. Still, there have been gross abuses. And I think the fundamental question is the one that Lord Bauer poses in his paper, that is, to what extent is coercion an overflow product of making services available? In situations where central governments set specified population goals, isn't there temptation to place noxious family planning pressures on individuals and families? That's the quandary defenders of family planning have to wrestle with. I don't think family planning efforts need become coercive, but there is a powerful tendency in that direction in the Third World programs. Perhaps one mission of a conference like this should be to try to suggest mechanisms by which voluntary services could be made available without pressing people in dishonorable and undemocratic ways.

MR. WATTENBERG: Mr. Hullander?

MR. HULLANDER: One of the benefits of such a rich discussion is that you can find something to agree with and something to disagree with on just about every issue.

Starting from the last, at AID we are very, very cognizant of the point you raise. A fundamental premise of our system is that programs be based on free and independent choice, and to avoid even the thought of coercion. So the presence of it, the hint of it, causes great alarm to us.

The choice of family planning, or the size of the family, is the individual's. We focus our efforts on informing that individual of the benefits as well as the costs, the alternatives, and the methods to make that choice. As part of that, it is our objective not to say what is the optimum number of children, what is the rational size, either for the family or the nation. It is pointed at getting whatever child is born to survive. So, much of our effort is in education and in health. The second part of our discussion is about the relationship between population and environment. The famine in Ethiopia is not particularly a matter of a quantum increase in population; it is a quantum decrease in agricultural production. Fifteen years ago when I was in those high plains, I saw corn that was the envy of Iowa. You don't see that today.

It was the policies that stopped agricultural production, stopped the availability of food per capita, that was a major precipitant of the famine that we have today.

MR. EBERSTADT: I don't hear the thought being expressed that population doesn't matter. What I hear being expressed is a healthy agnosticism. And I would like to second what other people have said in terms of congratulating the paper presenters and some of the discussants, because I think that what they have succeeded in doing is elevating the discussion to a new and higher level.

I think Julian Simon deserves a tremendous amount of credit for bringing to light in the last five or ten years some of the counterculture literature that has been around for a long time. You mentioned William Petty. I'm thinking of more recent contributions like Colin Clark or Ester Boserup, or Albert Hirschman. There has been for quite some time in the intellectual community this agnosticism, this debate. But some of the writing has taken place outside the United States, and we have tended to sweep it under the carpet.

It seems to me that what all of this does is to point very clearly to the need for additional dispassionate, objective, non-partisan research on the relationship between population growth and economic development, perhaps building up that body of research by taking a more or less case study approach.

MR. WATTENBERG: Gale Johnson.

MR. JOHNSON: I would like to discuss something that was in much of the public discussion at the time of the world conference in Mexico City. That is the relationship, alleged often, between rapid population growth and the growth of cities, particularly large cities. It seems "reasonable," in quotes, to assume that there is such a relationship. But there has been almost no work done on the effects of various policies upon the growth of the cities such as Mexico City, where the government of Mexico, as is the case in many other countries, significantly subsidizes people who live in the cities and then complains too many people live there. In Mexico City, public transportation is virtually free; food costs have been cut substantially for people who live in the cities, but

not in the country. It is not surprising that people move to Mexico City in large numbers and make it, in some people's minds—not those living there, necessarily—a very bad place to be.

". . . the relationship, alleged often, between rapid population growth and the growth of cities . . . seems "reasonable," in quotes . . . but . . . government . . . in many . . . countries significantly subsidizes people who live in the cities and then complains too many people live there."

D. Gale Johnson

But in addition to that, of course, the growth of cities is a phenomenon that is inextricably related to economic progress: It is not primarily population that induces cities to grow, but real per capita income gains. For example, India, which has had rapid population growth for the last 30 years, has not seen a significant shift in population from rural to urban areas, and, unfortunately, the reason is its per capita income growth has not been that great. Whereas other countries that have had not so large population growth have seen sharp increases in city size.

The distribution of population between the countryside and the city is a very complex phenomenon which requires much more investigation, particularly if we are to isolate the effects of government policies upon migration.

MR. WATTENBERG: Mr. Lal?

MR. LAL: I want to consider why, despite different answers to the question "Are world population trends a problem?" people end up with policy prescriptions that are very similar.

I think how one answers this type of question really does reflect one's *Weltanschauung*, and we have come across this here.

Certain people really do believe that the world can be planned, that it is feasible to plan the world, and we can identify in some sort of engineering sense precisely the costs and benefits of different outcomes, and we can control those.

Now, if you did a history of thought, of what people have thought about population, I would submit that you would probably find that population theorists have always developed models to fight the last battle. We know, for instance, that Malthus was absolutely right about what happened before we lived, and he was disproved, essentially, subsequently. Similarly, many people who are very upset about the population prob-

---

> "Certain people really do believe that the world can be planned, that . . . we can identify in some sort of engineering sense precisely the costs and benefits of different outcomes, and we can control those."
>
> **Deepak Lal**

---

lem are only projecting what they were seeing happening in the fifties and sixties.

You cannot have a theory of population growth, it seems to me, which is entirely independent of broader historical, sociological, or cultural analysis. How societies will react to population changes is not easily predicted. And, though retrospective historical studies of why populations behaved in one way or the other are fine, I am not at all convinced that much of the statistical evidence Mr. Fornos cited and someone else cited is of much relevance, because one of the few things I have learned in my years about econometric evidence is that it is always—and I insist, always—equivocal.

MR. WATTENBERG: Mr. Merrick?

MR. MERRICK: Yes, I hear two basic points being made, and I'd like some clarification on the second one. I hear some making the point that it is important not to attribute food problems and other development problems to population growth. I think there is general agreement on that point and the fact that that may have been exaggerated in the past. I certainly would agree with that view myself.

But I also think I hear the point being made, at least by innuendo, that more rapid population growth—and I'll take the specific example of the rate that has been approaching 4 percent per annum in Kenya—somehow does not aggravate Kenya's struggle to balance population and resources. And even that dealing with that stress would not be easier for the Kenyan government if population growth were perhaps 2½ percent rather than 4 percent.

I am pretty sure that the Kenyan government's perception is that it would be easier, and that a 4 percent population growth rate aggravates their problems. I don't think that they are under any illusions that lower population growth will solve their problems, but at least it would be easier to deal with them. And I think that those who would answer that 4 percent is better than 2½ percent ought to share with the rest of us their logic.

MR. WATTENBERG: We'll return to that.

MR. EBERSTADT: There is one question which I would like to raise with Lord Bauer, which has to do with the matter of contraceptives as a market item. I wonder if, though an item be not widely accepted through commercial markets, it might nonetheless be worth subsidizing to the general public. Might there not be such a thing as market failure involved in the wide diffusion of the contraceptives?

Contraceptives, unlike Coca-Cola, or unlike radios, are something which generally it takes two people to agree upon using. And it is more usually a family decision, and decisions made within the family may be subject to certain sorts of processes which aren't quite as simple as simply going out and buying goods which they will avail themselves of.

MR. WATTENBERG: At this point I would like to make a comment myself. We are always talking about the population problems and pressures, such as they may be, in the developing world.

> "I believe I am correct in saying that this is the first time in human history that the most powerful nations in the world have voluntarily set into motion a process which will lead to significant *reductions* in their national population."
>
> **Ben Wattenberg**

Yet, as I scan the data, what has interested me most about population trends in the modern world, what I must say I think is the most important problem—if that's the right word—is the advent of below-replacement fertility rates across almost the entire developed world. I believe I am correct in saying that this is the first time in human history that the most powerful nations in the world have voluntarily set into motion a process which will lead to significant reductions in national population. Malthus taught us that population growth is geometric, which it is, but so is population decline. There too is a population momentum that sets in.

Now, when you say the developed world, you can use that phrase almost—not quite—as a surrogate for the democratic world. If today people living in democratic nations in this troubled world of ours represent only one-fourth, roughly speaking, of the global population, by the end of the next century, at current fertility rates projected at medium levels, they will represent not one-fourth of the population, but only about one-tenth.

Now, one can say the United States and other democracies will still be very strong, and that raw numbers don't count—I am familiar with those arguments. But that is not clear. And if they survive at one-tenth, will they survive at one-twentieth, at one one-hundredth? Something important is happening, and it is not an easy process to reverse, because of demographic momentum.

I just wanted to go on record to present a new problem which I think the international population community, particularly in the democratic and developed worlds, ought to be most interested in. Not coincidentally, it is a topic I expect to be writing about soon at some length.

I know that Mr. Salas and Mr. Simon and Mr. Preston and Mr. Bauer want to issue their rejoinders, and then I hope we'll have time to go back to the panel for one more round.

Mr. Salas, please.

MR. SALAS: Thank you, Mr. Chairman.

I just want to make a comment on Mr. Simon's intervention. I want to assure the professor that I am not an advocate of centralized control or centralized views on population, and even if I wanted to I couldn't do it—for the simple reason, ladies and gentlemen, that the United Nations system is a collegial and a consensual body, which is not really controlled by any dominant group.

In both my statements here and my statement in Mexico, the very first thing I said was to respect national sovereignty and at the same time, to respect human and individual rights. That is the collective thinking of the United Nations. Population has to be reconciled between these two viewpoints.

"I am not an advocate of centralized control or centralized views on population, and even if I wanted to I couldn't do it—for the simple reason, ladies and gentlemen, that the United Nations system is a collegial and a consensual body. . . ."

Rafael Salas

Well, Professor Simon, I think, lifted several sentences from my statement. Where I agree with what he has been saying in his writings, I think he has not read to you. For instance, one paragraph before what he quoted here, I said, "The nature of population"—this is my speech in Mexico—"indicates that it is necessary to have both a time horizon and objective goal for the effective implementation of population policies and programs. Knowledge of its time paths is necessary to appreciate its relationships with ecological factors and their implications for a sustainable society. At any point in time, the sustainability of society is limited by the availability"—now, this is Simon—"of known resources, the rate of utilization, the levels of technology, and the financial, technical, and managerial constraints facing different countries." And this is even more Simon. "Within these time paths, it is of use that a few countries may in the short run

---

"In the long term, the balance between population size and sustainability is a moving equilibrium, determined . . . by changes in technological progress, resource discoveries and utilization, innovations in social organizations, and manifestations of human ingenuity."

Rafael Salas

---

have to increase their population for the optimum utilization of their resources. But all countries should aim"—that's where I go—"for a level of population in balance with their sustainable capacity. In the long term, the balance between population size and sustainability is a moving equilibrium, determined again here by changes in technological progress, resource discoveries and utilization, innovations in social organizations, and manifestations of human ingenuity."

What we are articulating to you is not our individual views in the secretariat. These are expressed views of countries. And as I said earlier, they vary from country to country. We have countries, for instance Catholic countries in Latin America, that only allow natural or rhythm methods for their family planning, and that has to be respected. I personally inaugurated the natural family planning clinic in Ecuador, to give you an ethical dimension of this. And that is the program of the government, that is supported by the government.

On the other hand, you have countries, of course, as have been cited here, like India and China, with large populations and different views. We have countries as I mentioned—like Mongolia, which want a pro-natalist policy. And the UN has to support that—although we have no techniques, really, except to lessen infant mortality and maternal morbidity and mortality.

In a sense, Professor Simon has to be thanked for many of his articles that show some of the deviations and simplistic assumptions about population programs. What I would only like to request of him is to take a look at the internal mechanisms of the UN system in terms of population assistance. In part of my paper I did not read I said, "At the end of this continuum is the individual, whose decisions and behavior are the most important of all. Individuals, not governments or institutions, make the final choices in the question of population. It follows that population policies should emphasize the problems and aspirations of individuals and their contribution to development."

Actually, the UN population program is people-oriented, rather than numbers.

Thank you.

MR. WATTENBERG: Thank you very much.

Julian Simon, I know you want to speak to what Mr. Salas has said. I would also be particularly interested in hearing your response to Mr.

Merrick's comments about population growth in Kenya at 4 percent versus 2.5 percent.

MR. SIMON: First, I would like to thank AEI for this meeting, because I think it really has been a most unusual opportunity for free exchange of a wide diversity of views, and I have found it valuable.

Mr. Salas says many things that I agree with and admire, and not just his quotes of me. If I have somehow quoted Mr. Salas's language in ways that do not reflect his thinking, I'll be very happy if he never uses again those phrases about population growth rates or population stabilization or government intervention, et cetera. And then, perhaps we will find that we are as close to being of one mind as Mr. Salas believes and hopes that we are—and I would like to be, also.

Now, on the matter of coercion, just very briefly—this is outside of my field—looking at the photographs in Steven Mosher's book, *Broken Earth*, of a seven-month pregnant woman being aborted in a forcible program in the village in which she lived strikes me as very compelling evidence of the eyes. And lest one doubt that Mosher is not representative, his book seems to jibe almost completely with the book by Fox Butterfield who is a *New York Times* representative and as much a member of the central establishment as anyone can be.

Now, let me go on to Tom Merrick, because I think he does deserve answers, both on the response of the population community in the past decades and on the rates of population growth in Kenya and elsewhere.

With respect to the response, including both commercial systems that have responded to the

---

"It strikes me that children by choice and not chance is one of the great goods in humanity, and I would guess that every single person in this room agrees."

Julian Simon

---

demand for contraception, as well as many government systems, I think they are very great human advances. It strikes me that children by choice and not chance is one of the great goods in humanity, and I would guess that every single person in this room agrees. And I agree with Karl Zinsmeister in applauding the humanitarian motives and the valuable outcomes of much of the work of that movement.

Now, as to population growth rates of, say, 4 percent or 2 percent. In the short run, children are a burden, and every parent knows that. We should recognize, however, that most of the burden of additional children is, in fact, carried by the parents themselves, though there is a burden upon society as well. And we do not know anything, so far as I know, scientifically, about whether the burden is disproportional when the growth rate is 4 percent or 2 percent, when a family has 10 children or 5 children. I don't know of any literature on this. I think that it would be a very valuable direction for research to go in.

But having said that there is a burden in the short run, we have to note that the benefits come in the long run, and do come. But those benefits in the long run are extremely difficult to quantify, because they are so extraordinarily indirect.

Werner Fornos talked of the deterioration of the quality of life. It is an unequivocal fact that two of the greatest miracles, perhaps the two greatest miracles in all of human history, have occurred in the past three centuries. One miracle was the rise in life expectancy in rich countries such as France, from a life expectancy at birth of less than 30 years for a woman in the middle of the 17th century, to well into the mid-70s at present. What greater miracle could there have been —and better health along with it?

And the second miracle is that in the three decades since World War II, life expectancy in the poor countries of the world has risen 15 or more years, and in China more than 20 years, to a life expectancy in the high-60s. All in a short two decades.

Those are unequivocal facts, and they both happened in the presence of the fastest population growth rates that humanity has ever known. I'll stop there.

MR. WATTENBERG: Sam Preston, and then Lord Bauer.

MR. PRESTON: Just a point on the last comment that Julian made. I think the causation is a bit curious there, that the population growth rates have risen as dramatically as they have, simply because life expectancy has increased as dramati-

cally as it has. By the way, in China it is a 40-year gain in life expectancy since 1930—quite incredible.

Two points in response to some things that have been said on developing countries. One, Peter Bauer is optimistic that people in developing countries have good knowledge of and access to family planning services from the private sector. I am less optimistic about that. I think Werner

---

" . . . the World Fertility Survey, conducted in some 40 countries, did very often reveal major amounts of ignorance about the possibilities for controlling one's own fertility."

Sam Preston

Fornos is correct to point out that the World Fertility Survey, conducted in some 40 countries, did very often reveal major amounts of ignorance about the possibilities for controlling one's own fertility. This should not surprise us. There is ignorance about many matters in developing countries. And I think that informational programs of the kind that family planning programs represent are an extraordinarily valuable tool in helping to modernize and helping to Westernize the developing world.

A second piece of evidence on that subject is that birth rate declines in a number of countries— not, perhaps, a majority of countries that have had family planning programs, but in a number of important ones—do seem to imply statistically a very close association between the intensification or the adoption of the family planning program and the reduction in the birth rate. Mexico, I think, is probably the clearest cut example of that, although one can always interpret time series differently. Maybe the birth rate would have fallen as sharply anyway. But I think there is a *prima facie* case that when family planning was vigorously adopted and pursued by the government around 1972, Mexico's birth rate started to decline from around 40 to perhaps 32 or 33 by the end of the decade. The prevalence of contraception among ever-married women increased from 10 percent during that period to about 38 percent, if I have the figures correctly. This to me implies that there was substantial unavailability of services prior to the government-sponsored family planning program.

One more point: AID's research budget, as I recall—and I saw the figures a couple of weeks ago—is somewhat less than 5 percent of the total budget at AID, and when you look at that 5 percent, much of it turns out not to be research on these basic issues that we are discussing today, but is spent on things like the RAPID program —a computerized tool—which many people have argued is not a research device at all, but a persuasional device, designed to convince governments of developing countries to reduce their rates of population growth.

In the state of flux and uncertainty we are currently in in this field, it is very important to fund research that will question some of the basic assumptions that we are using in our population funding programs.

MR. WATTENBERG: Lord Bauer.

LORD BAUER: I would like first to comment on the interesting point raised by Nick Eberstadt, and this is that decisions about fertility control or family size are made collectively by the family, and not by individuals, and that therefore, my analogy about the wide availability of cheap Western goods, consumer goods, and the lack of availability of cheap contraceptives in the same area, to some extent fails, because a purchase of the one is an individual decision, and the other is to some extent a family decision. This point raises very wide political and cultural matters.

Supposing that in certain societies, like the Islamic society, and to some extent South Asian societies, and others, the decisions about how many children to have depend largely on the man, not entirely, but largely. Now, this is con-

---

"Supposing that in certain societies, like the Islamic society, and to some extent South Asian societies, and others, the decisions about how many children to have depend largely on the man, not entirely, but largely. Now, this is contrary to our ethos, or to that of many people. Should we forcibly intervene?"

P. T. Bauer

---

trary to our ethos, or to that of many people. Should we forcibly intervene? People, particularly I regret to say in North America, and now increasingly also in Britain, think—whatever their pretenses—that it is perfectly in order to try and forcibly modify the cultures of others. Now, this raises a very wide issue; I will simply mention it.

Second are the problems—this, Mr. Merrick raised—of the Kenyan government: wouldn't it be a lot simpler for them to improve the standard of living if the rate of population growth were 2½ percent as distinct from 4 percent? Now, here, it all depends what you mean by the problems of the government of Kenya.

I regret to say I think these phrases are bandied about in an extremely facile fashion. If you mean by it that the objective of the Kenyan government is to increase real income per head, they would not have thrown out the Asians and

---

". . . if, as it seems to me a number of people in this room believe, you think the governments in the Third World act in the interest of their populations, there is something to learn."

P. T. Bauer

---

the Europeans who (a) have incomes way above the average, and (b) represent the most advancing elements in society, and are agents of modernization in those countries.

And if, as it seems to me a number of people in this room believe, you think the governments in the Third World act in the interest of their populations, there is something to learn. Their primary interest is to remain in power, to emasculate their opponents as best they can. It is not all that different in the West, either, only more pronounced in the Third World.

Now, I did not say in my paper that 6 million people were compulsively sterilized in India. What I said was that 6 million were sterilized, and very large numbers of them, compulsorily. I refer you to a September 1984 article by Dr. Paul Demeny of the Population Council, called "Bucharest, Mexico City, and Beyond." I was very surprised to read it, and the figures are taken from there. And if there are people who seriously believe that there was no coercion in India at the

Ambassador Clare Boothe Luce and Father James Schall

time—I've got this much literature on it—or that there is not in China, I can only answer what someone said when she saw the Duke of Welling-

---

"I assume that the purpose of population control is to make, or to help, poor people become richer."

Clare Boothe Luce

---

ton arm-in-arm with a Mrs. Jones: "Mr. Jones, I believe." If you believe that, you will believe anything.

MR. WATTENBERG: Mrs. Luce?

MRS. LUCE: I would like to say that I think this a very extraordinary meeting. The last time I put my mind seriously to this question, 20 years ago, it was being approached in terms of a certain choice that faced us, between population control and nuclear explosion. That was where the question stood. It certainly does not stand there today in the minds of the majority of this panel.

But I must note that, in listening carefully to these experts, I find that I am constantly thrown by the words "developed" and "underdeveloped." I think they are euphemisms for the richer and relatively poorer countries, or if you prefer,

the poor and the relatively richer countries. And I assume that the purpose of population control, which Mr. Salas reassures me is people-oriented—I am glad to hear that—I assume that the purpose of population control is to make, or to help, the poor people become richer.

What, I wonder, do the rich countries have that the poor countries don't? Having spent the summer in Switzerland, it certainly isn't resources, either human—in terms of numbers—or the riches of the land—which Switzerland, like Japan, does not have. Many of the poor countries do have resources and do not seem to be able to exploit them.

Now, why don't they exploit their resources? Why do they starve, as Peter Bauer tells us, in countries where they have plenty of agricultural possibilities?

Well, it seems to me very simple that the reason is that the people themselves don't have freedom, that is to say democracy, and they don't have industrialization, which is the miracle that happened two centuries ago. They don't have either capitalism or freedom, democracy or an economic system fit for free men.

Now, as long as these countries remain not free, it seems to me regardless of their resources, they'll be exploited by their tyrants and their rulers.

It is interesting to reflect, when you speak of

food, that Russia in the year 1900 exported 40 percent of its food products. Today, it would starve or would have serious food difficulties without the assistance of American agriculture.

In any event, I think the trouble I am encountering today is that we are not being quite honest when we discuss the population problem unless we put it into the context of the economic and the political situations in the countries at issue.

We must, it seems, pledge ourselves not to interfere, not to persuade the people against their political systems, and at the same time help them solve problems which can't be solved until they do change their systems.

MR. WATTENBERG: Thank you very much. Mr. Espenshade?

MR. ESPENSHADE: Just one quick observation, in line with your earlier point about problems of low fertility in developed countries. One of the most

---

"One of the most startling [population] statistics I think I have ever seen . . . is that the developed countries . . . as a whole have fertility rates below replacement, which would mean that in the absence of international migration patterns, these countries would eventually die out."

Tom Espenshade

---

startling statistics I think I have ever seen on the World Population Data Sheet that the Population Reference Bureau puts out is that the developed countries, as they are defined there, as a whole have fertility rates below replacement, which would mean that in the absence of international migration patterns, these countries would eventually die out. And that's the problem that you are pointing to.

MR. WATTENBERG: That's exactly the problem that I am pointing out.

MR. ESPENSHADE: Just a brief comment. One has to also take into account the fact that these countries are gaining immigrants from poorer nations, and that if you took that process into account, then in the long term, never mind defin-

ing how long that would be, you end up with populations that are of constant size in those developed countries with fertility rates below replacement.

MR. WATTENBERG: Yes, but you may end up with a Turkish population and culture in West Germany, which is not what they are actually after.

MR. ESPENSHADE: Right. Now, my main point is what that points to in the whole process of assimilation, acculturation, integration, whatever you want to call it. What happens to these folks when they come into a new situation—to what extent do they and their immigrant descendants retain values and attitudes from the countries that they have come from? To what extent do they gradually become acculturated, integrated into the new society? That seems to be the fundamental issue there.

MR. WATTENBERG: Our time is almost up.

We have dealt with a variety of technical aspects of the alleged problem of population growth in the less-developed countries; about whether contraceptives are available or not available, how fast the growth rates are, and so forth and so on. And there are, as we expected, two points of view about whether current population trends are a problem or not.

My sense is that when you have that kind of a polarization of viewpoint, there is more than just technical disagreement. Somewhere around such technical arguments, one usually finds ideology.

And what I would like to do, just as a final round robin to close the discussion is to take final one-sentence comments suggesting what it is that we are really disagreeing about.

MR. EBERSTADT: Yes. To what extent should individuals and families be allowed to make decisions that their government thinks are wrong?

MR. WATTENBERG: Okay.
Yes?

MR. MERRICK: My answer is almost the same as his. To what extent is it appropriate, and then under what circumstances, for governments to intervene in what many regard as the rights of individuals to make reproductive choices?

MR. WATTENBERG: Are we saying it is a freedom argument, it is a planning argument? Is that it?

MR. MERRICK: Individual versus social choices, yes.

MR. WATTENBERG: Yes?

MR. LAL: I would say the Aristotelian versus the Enlightenment view of man.

MR. WATTENBERG: Julian?

MR. SIMON: Two things. First, attitudes and values about human life *per se*, and the value of human life versus other species such as the dolphins. Second, views of the market versus planning, the Anglo-Saxon notion of freedom versus the Marxian notion of freedom.

MR. WATTENBERG: Werner?

MR. FORNOS: I'm sorry. I think the issue that we are arguing over is our right to exploit the hungry masses of the world, instead of working for a betterment of the world. I mean, we continue to worry about whether only 10 percent of the world will be democratized. Do you not recognize India as a democracy? Do you not believe that we are going to export democracy in the next 20 years? Have you no hope for democracy spreading throughout the world?

MR. WATTENBERG: I have a great deal of hope. I don't know what is going to happen. And I think your point about India is quite interesting. I was talking about industrialized democracies. But that's an interesting addition.

MR. ZINSMEISTER: My answer would follow on that. Democracy is only possible where rights are vested in the correct places. If you vest rights in a small planning oligarchy at the top of the country, you don't have a democracy. If you vest rights in the individuals, you have a democracy. So the point made earlier that we are really arguing about the level at which rights are properly vested is, it seems to me, the correct one.

MR. WATTENBERG: Meeting closed. Thank you all very much.

Statistical Appendix

Demographic Indicators
1950-1985

TABLE A-1
TOTAL FERTILITY RATE (TFR)[a] FOR WORLD AND REGIONS

	1950-55	1980-85	Goal for population stability[b]	Decline in TFR since 1950-55 as percent of total decline needed to reach population stability
	(lifetime children per woman)		(lifetime children per woman)	
World	5.0	3.6	2.1	48%
More-developed countries	2.8	2.0	2.1	114
Less-developed countries	6.2	4.1	2.1	51
Africa	6.5	6.4	2.1	2
Caribbean	5.2	3.4	2.1	58
Central America	6.8	4.8	2.1	43
Temperate So. America	3.5	3.2	2.1	21
Tropical So. America	6.4	4.1	2.1	53
Asia	6.0	3.6	2.1	61
East Asia	5.5	2.3	2.1	94
South Asia	6.4	4.7	2.1	40

NOTE: The total fertility rate (TFR) is among the more refined demographic measures. Unlike growth rates and crude birth rates, it measures fertility trends without the distortions created by prior population developments. It measures what is actually happening among families. It may be seen that the more-developed nations have already gone below population stability and that the less-developed nations have gone roughly half the way toward achieving population stability.

[a]The TFR is the average number of children that would be born per woman per lifetime at current birth rates.
[b]Assumes mortality levels will continue to decline, and absence of net immigration.
SOURCE: U.S. Bureau of the Census based on United Nations 1982 Assessment of World Population Prospects.

TABLE A-2
INFANT MORTALITY RATE
(infant deaths per 1,000 live births)

	1950-55	1980-85	Percent Change
World	139	81	−42
More developed	56	17	−70
Less developed	159	92	−42
Africa	185	115	−38
Caribbean	124	58	−53
Central America	122	57	−53
Temperate So. America	83	37	−55
Tropical So. America	136	70	−49
Asia	155	87	−44
East Asia	124	36	−71
South Asia	182	109	−40

SOURCE: United Nations 1982 assessment of world population prospects.

TABLE A-3
LIFE EXPECTANCY AT BIRTH
(years)

	1950-55	1980-85	Gain In Years	Percent Gain
World	45.8	58.9	+13.1	29
More developed	65.1	73.0	+ 7.9	12
Less developed	41.0	56.6	+15.6	38
Africa	37.5	49.7	+12.2	33
Caribbean	51.9	64.0	+12.1	23
Central America	49.3	65.0	+15.7	32
Temperate So. America	60.3	69.0	+ 8.7	14
Tropical So. America	49.9	62.9	+13.0	26
Asia	41.2	57.9	+16.7	41
East Asia	42.5	68.0	+25.5	60
South Asia	40.1	53.6	+13.5	34

SOURCE: U.S. Bureau of the Census based on United Nations 1982 Assessment of world population prospects.

TABLE A-4
EDUCATION INDICATORS IN DEVELOPING COUNTRIES

Primary School Enrollment
(Percent of age group)

	1960	1981
Low income countries	80%	94%
Middle income countries	75	102[a]

[a] Percent may be over 100 if children outside primary school ages are enrolled in primary school.

Secondary School Enrollment
(Percent of age group)

	1960	1981
Low income countries	18%	34%
Middle income countries	14	41

Enrollment in Higher Education
(Percent of persons 20-24 years old)

	1960	1981
Low income countries	2%	4%
Middle income countries	3	11

SOURCE: *World Development Report 1984.*

TABLE A-5
ADULT LITERACY RATE IN DEVELOPING COUNTRIES
(percent)

	1960	1970	Around 1980
Low income countries	25%	30%	51%
Middle income countries	48	63	65
All developing countries	39	45	56

SOURCE: World Bank. *World Tables,* 3rd. edition, 1983.

TABLE A-6
HEALTH-RELATED INDICATORS IN DEVELOPING COUNTRIES

	1960	1980
Physicians per 100,000 people		
Low-income countries	8.3	17.3
Middle-income countries	5.8	18.5
Nurses per 100,000 people		
Low-income countries	13.8	20.7
Middle-income countries	26.1	53.0

SOURCE: U.S. Bureau of the Census based on *World Development Report, 1984.*

TABLE A-7
CALORIE SUPPLY PER CAPITA IN DEVELOPING COUNTRIES
(Percentage of "daily requirement")

	1960	1970	Around 1980
Low-income countries	87%	90%	97%
Middle-income countries	100	101	110

SOURCE: World Bank. *World Tables,* 3rd. edition, 1983.

TABLE A-8
GROWTH OF GNP PER CAPITA IN DEVELOPING COUNTRIES

	GNP Per Capita (1985 U.S. dollars)	
	1960	1982
Low-income countries	$160	$ 310
Middle-income countries	761	1680

SOURCE: *World Development Report 1984.*

TABLE A-9
ANNUAL WESTERN AID TO DEVELOPING COUNTRIES[a]
(billions of 1985 U.S. dollars)

1960	1970	1980
$21.2	$23.5	$35.3

[a] This is official aid only and does not include massive capital transfers to LDC's via private bank lending, export credits, private and corporate investment, and so forth.

SOURCE: Organization for Economic Cooperation and Development.

Further Reading

Bauer, Lord P. T.—*Dissent on Development*, Harvard University Press (Cambridge, MA, 1976).
—*Equality, the Third World, and Economic Delusion*, Harvard University Press (Cambridge, MA, 1981).

Boserup, Ester.—*The Conditions of Agricultural Growth*, George Allen and Unwin (London, 1965).

Clark, Colin.—*The Myth of Overpopulation*, Lumen Christi Press (Houston, 1975).
—"Population Growth and Productivity," in *Research in Population Economics*, Vol. I, JAI Press (Greenwich, CT, 1978).

Easterlin, Richard, and Eileen Crimmins.—*The Fertility Revolution: A Supply-Demand Analysis*, University of Chicago Press (Chicago, forthcoming 1985).

Kelley, Allen, with Timothy King.—*The New Population Debate*, Population Reference Bureau (Washington, DC, 1985).

McNamara, Robert.—"Time Bomb or Myth: The Population Problem," *Foreign Affairs*, Summer 1984.

Preston, Samuel, contributor.—*Report of the Committee on Population of the National Research Council*, National Academy of Sciences (Washington, DC, forthcoming 1985).

Salas, Rafael.—*Reflections on Population*, Pergamon Press (New York, 1984).

Schall, James, S.J.—*Human Dignity and Human Numbers*, Alba House (Staten Island, NY, 1971).
—*Welcome Number 4,000,000,000*, Alba Books (Canfield, OH, 1977).

Simon, Julian.—*The Economics of Population Growth*, Princeton University Press (Princeton, NJ, 1977).
—*The Ultimate Resource*, Princeton University Press (Princeton, NJ, 1981).

U.S. Dept. of State, *Report of the United States Delegation to the U.N. International Conference on Population*, 1984. (Includes, as appendix, official U.N. Report on conference proceedings.)

Wattenberg, Ben.—*The Good News is The Bad News is Wrong*, Simon and Schuster (New York, 1984).

World Bank.—*World Development Report 1984*, Oxford University Press (New York, 1984).

About the Editors

Ben Wattenberg is a Senior Fellow at the American Enterprise Institute and was a member of the U.S. Delegation to the 1984 World Population Conference in Mexico City. He is the author of a series of books on U.S. demographic trends, the latest of which is entitled *The Good News is The Bad News is Wrong*.

Karl Zinsmeister is a demographic and economic researcher at AEI, and a national commentator on demographic subjects for Radio America. He attended the Mexico City population conference as a journalist.